EMERSON
and the Art of the Diary

EMERSON
and the Art of the Diary

Lawrence Rosenwald

New York   Oxford
OXFORD UNIVERSITY PRESS
1988

PS
1631
R67
1988

Oxford University Press

Oxford   New York   Toronto
Delhi   Bombay   Calcutta   Madras   Karachi
Petaling Jaya   Singapore   Hong Kong   Tokyo
Nairobi   Dar es Salaam   Cape Town
Melbourne   Auckland

and associated companies in
Berlin   Ibadan

Copyright © 1988 by Oxford University Press, Inc.

Published by Oxford University Press, Inc.
200 Madison Avenue, New York, New York 10016

Oxford is a registered trademark of Oxford University Press

Library of Congress Cataloging-in-Publication Data
Rosenwald, Lawrence Alan, 1948–
Emerson and the art of the diary / Lawrence Rosenwald.
p.   cm.
Includes index.
ISBN 0-19-505333-8
1. Emerson, Ralph Waldo, 1803–1882—Diaries.
2. Emerson, Ralph Waldo, 1803–1882—Style.
3. Authors, American—19th century—Diaries—History and criticism.
4. Autobiography.
I. Title.
PS1631.R67 1988   818'.303—dc19   [B]   87-23074   CIP

246897531

Printed in the United States of America
on acid-free paper

58585

FOR CYNTHIA

Is there any other work for the poet but a good journal?
Thoreau, *Journal* X: 115

Why rake up old MSS to find therein a man's soul? You do not look for conversation in a corpse.
Emerson, *Journals and Miscellaneous Notebooks* V: 337

Acknowledgments

No doubt I've forgotten valuable help I've received, and I apologize to any neglected benefactors. But I remember many with pleasure. My thanks, for gracious and scrupulous readings of all or part of this, to Quentin Anderson, Sharon Cameron, Phyllis Cole, Julie Cumming, Arthur Gold, Maurice Gonnaud, Tim Peltason, David Pillemer, Monica Raymond, Gail Reimer, Bob Stein, and the members of the Wellesley College Colloquium on the History of Ideas. The editors of *The Journals and Miscellaneous Notebooks of Ralph Waldo Emerson* (JMN) have by their superb edition made this work possible. A briefer version of the first chapter appeared in *Raritan Review;* both it and the present version have benefited from the expert editing of Richard Poirier. Joel Myerson provided authoritative bibliographical help. Wellesley College funded a year's leave. Special thanks to Margery Sabin, who read the whole manuscript, helped me get rid of its pedantic clarifications, and showed me by her more literary criticisms what sort of a book I wanted to write and what sort I didn't, and how to make that clearer to my readers. Finally, my deepest thanks to Sacvan Bercovitch, friend and teacher, who more than any other scholar gave me the courage to pursue what in bleaker moments seemed an obsessive and peripheral interest.

Preface

In November of 1984, Harold Bloom published in the *New York Review of Books* an article about Emerson called "Mr. America." The title promises, and the article performs, a canonization; the canonization marks a moment in our history. We have freed ourselves from the sage of Concord, the bland and simplistic optimist; in his place we have found our contemporary, a precursor and spiritual colleague of Nietzsche, a living writer of great power and interest, the man Bloom describes as the "inescapable theorist of virtually all subsequent American writing."[1] This is all to the good, and Bloom in this article and elsewhere[2] has demonstrated by the quality of his attention to Emerson just how much we have to gain from such a conception. But while deliberately driving nails into the coffin of one false Emerson, Bloom offhandedly tidies the bust of another; he does away with Emerson the fuzzy thinker but retains Emerson the failed artist, writing that "[Emerson's] true genre was no more the lecture than it had been the sermon . . . and certainly not the essay, though that is his only formal achievement, besides a double handful of strong poems."[3] This reflects the most tenacious of all our beliefs about Emer-

1. "Mr. America," *New York Review of Books* 21: 18, November 22, 1984, 19.
2. "The Freshness of Transformation: or Emerson on Influence," ATQ 21: 45–56 (also in David Levin, ed., *Emerson: Prophecy, Metamorphosis, and Influence* [New York: Columbia University Press, 1975], pp. 129–48, and *A Map of Misreading* [New York: Oxford University Press], pp. 160–92); and "Emerson: The Self-Reliance of American Romanticism," in *Figures of Capable Imagination* (New York: Continuum, 1976), pp. 46–64.
3. Bloom, "Mr. America," p. 20.

son, and in his expression of it Bloom leaves us where we began, a hundred years ago, with Matthew Arnold's judgment "we have not in Emerson a great poet, a great writer . . . [but] a friend and aider of those who would live in the spirit."[4] The strongest critics between Arnold and Bloom only elaborate that judgment. Henry James writes in 1887 that

> Emerson had his message, but he was a good while looking for his form—the form which, as he himself would have said, he never completely found and of which it was rather characteristic of him that his later years (with their growing refusal to give him the *word*), wishing to attack him in his most vulnerable point, where his tenure was least complete, had in some degree the effect of despoiling him. . . . He is a striking exception to the general rule that writings live in the last resort by their form; that they owe a large part of their fortune to the art with which they have been composed. It is hardly too much, or too little, to say of Emerson's writings in general that they were not composed at all.[5]

F. O. Matthiessen brusquely rejects the Jamesian paradox, writing straightforwardly in 1941 that "Emerson never created a form great enough to ensure that his books will continue to be read."[6]

Now we can easily enough make sense of a man who is both a fuzzy thinker and a failed writer. But what can it mean to have as the inescapable theorist of our writing a man who was not essentially a writer at all?

Curiously, Bloom himself hints at the answer; later in the same article he writes that "Emerson's journals are his authentic work."[7] This sentence lies inert, and is not brought into combination with Bloom's disparagement of Emerson *qua* writer; but perhaps it can be, and perhaps then it can help us out of our muddle. To begin, we have only to take the step of positing that a writer's authentic work is after all likely to be among his formal achievements, indeed likely to be his true genre. That I believe to be the case: that Emerson's journals are his authentic work, his greatest formal achievement, his true and adequate genre. But to argue as much is difficult, because the argu-

---

4. Arnold, "Emerson," in *Discourses in America* (London: Macmillan, 1889), pp. 178–79.
5. James, "Emerson," in F. O. Matthiessen, *The James Family*, (New York: Knopf, 1947), pp. 441, 452–53.
6. Matthiesen, *American Renaissance* (New York: Oxford University Press, 1968), p. 75
7. Bloom, "Mr. America," p. 20.

ment entails assessing a literary masterpiece in a form that we have come to consider a literary form only very recently.

Let us suppose that a reader living in a world dominated by Poe's dictum that a true poem must be readable in an hour were somehow to get interested in the *Prelude*. He would read, but only be frustrated by, scholars' passing, causal, concessive tributes to the power of that (essentially autobiographical or essayistic) text. He might, if he were venturesome, attempt to argue that a composition in verse of many thousand lines might actually be construed as a *poem;* finally he might set out, tentatively and exploratorily, to consider what sort of poem it might be.

This hypothesized world is no more misguided than our own. A large selection from Emerson's journals was published in ten volumes between 1909 and 1914. A selection from them made by Bliss Perry (and distributed by the Book-of-the-Month Club) came out in 1926. They were published again, this time almost in their entirety, in a form as faithful to the original as a book can come to a manuscript without being a facsimile, between 1960 and 1978. An illuminating section from them made by Joel Porte came out in 1982. It is nonetheless the case that no literary study of them has ever been made.

Accordingly, I propose to make a first, preparatory description of one of the great masterpieces of American writing. My goal, to use Sharon Cameron's language in her brilliant and original study of Thoreau's journal, is to "open the *Journal* for public scrutiny."[8] The description is articulated in four sections. The first is a methodological prologue on reading diaries, or more precisely on the beliefs we hold that inhibit our reading of diaries and on the program for diary reading that we can derive from looking hard at those beliefs. The remaining sections attempt to carry out that program. The second section, treating Emerson's journals between 1819 and 1833, is an essay on how Emerson the diarist finds his form. The third and longest section comprises five chapters on the form Emerson found: an introduction; a comparison between the journal and Emerson's own lectures and essays; a comparison between the journal and other Transcendentalist journals; a comparison between the journal and the German aphorism book; and a comparison between the journal and quotation books, for example, Montaigne's *Essays* and Eckermann's *Conversations with Goethe*. The last section is an account of how Emerson lost the form

8. Cameron, *Writing Nature* (New York: Oxford University Press, 1985), p. 15.

he had found; it discusses the decay of the journal in the context of the peculiar character of Emerson's old age.

These individual sections can be conceived of in various groupings. First, a methodological prologue followed by a narrative of the progress of Emerson the diarist from beginning to middle to end. Second, a methodological prologue followed by two different sorts of studies, one diachronic and one synchronic. This second conception may make better sense of the actual relation between the third section and the sections preceding and following it; for though these latter do in fact treat portions of the journal preceding and following the portion treated in the third, they also treat them from a different viewpoint. The second and fourth sections look at the progress of Emerson's art over time, the third at the nature of his art at an imagined moment of stasis. That moment is a fiction, of course; the progress of Emerson's art never stops. But equally a fiction is the notion that in that progress nothing remains fixed, and the fiction of stasis is necessary to describe certain of the journal's powers and excellences. In this perspective the third section is not so much a bridge from the second to the fourth as a complement to both; both the second and fourth sections, on the one hand, and the third, on the other, offer *independent* accounts of the nature of Emerson's diaristic art, and the divergences between them result precisely from the divergence in viewpoint from which they originate.

The third of the possible groupings raises a different question. The first section proposes a program for reading diaries both as expressive documents and as works of art. The second and third sections seem chiefly occupied with the diary as a work of art, the fourth with the diary as expressive document. This is, in fact, largely the case, not least because the fourth is occupied with the stretch of Emerson's diary that is least interesting when read as a work of art. But it is also true that the two perspectives are intertwined throughout, or rather that throughout the ensuing account Emerson's formal artistry is taken as being itself the expression of his general *intelligence,* an intelligence within which artistic and personal needs are inextricable from one another.

> I propose to myself to read Schiller of whom I hear much. What shall I read? His Robbers? oh no, for that was the crude fruit of his immature mind. He thought little of it himself. What then: his Aesthetics? oh no, that is only his struggle with Kantian metaphysics. His poetry? oh no, for he was a poet only by study. His histories? And so with all his

productions, they were fermentations by which his mind was working itself clear, they were the experiments by which he got his skill and the fruit, the bright pure gold of all was—Schiller himself.

In thinking about Emerson and his journals I have come back again and again to this passage. It is not, I think, a denial of the human interest of the work of art but an assertion of the esthetic interest of the human life itself considered as an artifact, perhaps the supreme artifact, among many. The present book is written to articulate that interest also.

Wellesley, Massachusetts   L. R.
October 1987

Contents

I

Prolegomena

The great English and American diaries are among the most highly
regarded and yet systematically neglected of all literary texts. We
agree, in conversation or in remarks written *en passant*, that these
texts are major works of literature and their authors, major artists; but
when doing literary criticism we do not write about them. We have,
to be sure, the various intelligent small studies of Virginia Woolf's
The Common Reader, of Robert Fothergill's *Private Chronicles*, of
Thomas Mallon's *A World of Their Own*. But we have no books even
on Pepys's diary, or on Boswell's, or on Byron's; nor any on Dorothy
Wordsworth's, Sir Walter Scott's, Benjamin Haydon's, Francis Kil-
vert's, or Katherine Mansfield's. Of the great American diaries, Thoreau's is the object both of Perry Miller's *Consciousness in Concord*
and of Sharon Cameron's remarkable *Writing Nature;* but Samuel
Sewall's, Aaron Burr's, Bronson Alcott's, even Emerson's have occa-
sioned only comments in passing, worshipful quotation, and deferen-
tial silence.[1]

1. On European diaries see Michele Leleu, *Les Journaux intimes* (Paris: Presses
Universitaires de France, 1952); Gustav René Hocke, *Das Europaeische Tagebuch*
(Wiesbaden: Limes, 1963); Alain Girard, *Les Journaux intimes* (Paris: Presses Universitaires de France, 1963); Uwe Schultz, ed., *Das Tagebuch und der moderne Autor*
(Frankfurt am Main: Ullstein, 1965); Peter Boerner, *Tagebuch* (Stuttgart: Metzger,
1969); V. Del Litto, ed., *Le Journal intime et ses formes litteraires: Actes du Colloque
de septembre 1975* (Geneva: Droz, 1978). The best of these are Girard, Boerner, and
Del Litto; Boerner and Hocke contain extensive bibliographies, Hocke also a rich
anthology.

The relative abundance of material rightly suggests that European diaries have fared
a little better than their English and American counterparts—but only a little. As the

But though we are reticent to speak of diaries as works of art, we are eager to speak of them as testimonies of character, and quick to trust them in that capacity; biographers and historians and psychologists present themselves before diaries as devout Greeks presented themselves before oracles. Examples of an endemic practice are pointless; the best evidence of this widespread habit is the common formulae by which the testimony of diaries is introduced, formulae that once isolated easily reveal the weakness of their underlying assumptions, "if we want to see what P really thought of Q, we have only to consult the pertinent entries in her diary"; "F himself makes the matter perfectly clear, writing in his diary that . . ."; "X reveals the deep motivation of the work in a contemporary diary entry, writing that . . . ." Here and there a skeptic turns up: Léon Brunschvicg, hating Rousseau, declares in *De la connaissance de soi* that introspection leads us not towards but away from a knowledge of the self; Walter Scott confronts the first appearance of Pepys's diary in 1825 with the judicious caution of a lawyer and a man of the world.[2] But for the most part we take diarists at their word, knowing perfectly well that we cannot take living men and women so if we are to survive. Our critical diffidence is surely an error; our psychological credulity is no less so.

I take it that both errors proceed from our deep beliefs regarding diaries. I take it also that these beliefs are the more deeply held for having been only shallowly examined, retaining their tenacious hold on us below the level of critical consciousness, assumptions rather than conclusions, acted on rather than thought about. Accordingly, this essay attempts to identify, to assess, and to modify these beliefs. It is divided into four parts. The first is a definition. The remaining might be called: The Diary as Artifact; The Diary as Testimony; The Diary as Literature; they might also be called, more pointedly: Against the Myth of Privacy; Against the Myth of Veridicality; Against the Myth of Artlessness.

---

titles suggest, all these books start from scratch, taking up the fundamental problems from the beginning; none of them except Girard's pursues a specific historical investigation, and neither these books nor any other offers a comprehensive literary study of any major European diarist.

2. Brunschvicg, *De la connaissance de soi* (Paris: Presses Universitaires de France, 1931), p. 8; Scott, "Pepys's Memoirs" *Quarterly Review* 33: (1825–26), pp. 281–314.

I

We can best define the diary by taking over the Russian Formalist distinction between form and function[3] and by positing that genres can in general be described as certain forms and certain functions occurring in combination. In form a diary is a chronologically ordered sequence of dated entries addressed to an unspecified audience. We call that form a diary when a writer uses it to fulfill certain functions. We might describe those functions collectively as the discontinuous[4] recording of aspects of the writer's own life; more technically we might say that to call a text of the proper form a diary we must posit a number of identities: between the author and the narrator; between the narrator and the principal character; and between the depicted and the real, this latter including the identity between date of entry and date of composition.[5]

Some annotations are necessary. First, "identity" ought not to be confused with resemblance. We need not believe that the person Emerson's diary describes resembles exactly or even very closely the "real" Emerson; we might say that a better description of the "real" Emerson is to be found in his essay "The Transcendentalist." In positing identity we mean simply that if Emerson writes in the diary that

3. See Oswald Ducrot and Tzvetan Todorov, *Dictionnaire encyclopédique des sciences du langage* (Paris: du Seuil, 1972), pp. 189–91.

4. "Discontinuous" is deliberately vague. Some diarists write entries on the dates assigned; some diarists write a number of entries at a stretch, Pepys and Boswell among them, and clearly we ought not to formulate a definition excluding them. But as clearly we would not call a diary a text written from a single retrospective viewpoint.

5. See on this matter Phillippe Lejeune, *Le Pacte autobiographique* (Paris: du Seuil, 1975). Lejeune's book has greatly influenced my sense of the diary as a literary genre, but I have been unable to retain much of his terminology. Lejeune understands the identities noted in the text as making up what he calls the autobiographical contract. He describes this contract as being offered to the reader by the author in the text, in particular on the title page. "Poetry and Truth: From My Life, by Johann Wolfgang von Goethe" would thus be an announcement of genre, a declaration of authorship, and an offer of a deal.

Now the reader of a diary must believe that the identities the autobiographical contract purportedly guarantees are in fact true. But many diarists do not offer them; few diaries have authorial title pages, many as we have them begin in mid-course, and of those which we believe we have the whole, many begin without a declaration of intent. So the author often offers us nothing. We might, of course, describe ourselves as concluding a contract with an editor or a press, or with a manuscripts librarian, or with ourselves; but it makes better sense, I think, to speak not of contracts but of propositions we must *believe*. To read a diary *qua* diary we must posit or ascertain the identities Lejeune sees the autobiographical contract as guaranteeing.

such-and-such was the case, and we come across evidence to the contrary, we can say that Emerson was mistaken or a liar; neither statement can be made of the portrait putatively offered by the essay.

The phrase "about his or her own life" is deliberately and polemically left vague.[6] It is intended generally to allow the definition to conform to the wild diversity of actual diaries; in particular it is intended to exclude any reference to the self. At one moment or another the diary may take on the supplementary functions of introspection or itinerary or confession; none of these functions is intrinsic to it. It is, to be sure, normally a book of the self in the sense that one person keeps it and not many, and in those cases it is also a *revelation* of the self, in the sense that any action is, whether dealing cards or tying shoes; but it certainly need not be centrally occupied with a *description* of the self, or a narration of the self's activity. It may be a book of court gossip, or remarkable providences, or gleanings from other books, or notes on the weather.

But it must be a book of time; hence the deliberately and polemically cumbersome description of the form, and the final and perhaps redundant qualification in the description of the function. The diary, the *journal*, the *Tagebuch*, the *ephemerides* must be conceived as a book of days and dates and intervals. Whatever functions a diary serves, the writer of it chooses for them a form articulated by dates in chronological order, and a mode of writing spaced over time.

What neighboring genres does this definition exclude? Obviously, letter books, autobiographies, and diary fictions; less obviously but more pointedly, the nearer neighbors of authors' notebooks: Coleridge's and Hawthorne's, Lichtenberg's and Kafka's and Canetti's, Simone Weil's and Antonio Gramsci's. This is often a *felt* distinction, in that many authors, Lichtenberg and Von Platen and Kafka among them, keep works of both sorts, evidently finding the distinction necessary in their personal literary economy. More importantly, it is a distinction corresponding to our practice, to what we actually do when we read. Lacking even chronological succession, as we do in Coleridge's notebooks, we have no sense of necessary order within

6. Compare Elizabeth Bruss, *Autobiographical Acts* (Baltimore: Johns Hopkins University Press, 1976), p. 14: "aside from stating that some portions of the subject matter must concern the identity of the author, I have placed no further restriction on the subject matter, not even to stipulate whether autobiography must concern the 'inner' or the 'outer' man or devote more time to the delineation of the self than to others. . . . I believe that more delicate distinctions cannot be made without reference to far less broad literary contexts."

the text; nothing keeps us from shuffling the various items around, since nothing holds them in place, and nothing authorizes our deep inclination to read the text as a sequence.[7] Lacking dating, we have no sense of the text's necessary reference to the world outside it; an undated sequence of entries is formally an event taking place exclusively within the author's mind. A date ties a passage to history; in a diary every entry can be compared with the world outside it, the date of the entry indicating both a stage of the writer's life and a moment in the history of the world, and authorizing us to compare what has been written with what might have been written but was not.

"The sea-anemone," wrote Lichtenberg, "is half plant, half animal; man is half body and half spirit: always you find the most extraordinary creatures at the boundaries." In the world of the diary the amphibious creature is the diary edited for publication by its author. Bruce Frederick Cummings seems to have invented the species; he published in 1919 an edited version of much of his brilliant and moving diary as *Journal of a Disappointed Man*, under the pseudonym Barbellion. In 1921, after his death, the diary he had kept since the preparation of the earlier manuscript was published as *Last Journal*. Surely if as readers we permit ourselves to take account of information about composition we cannot read the two texts in the same way; both are composed of material written discontinuously, but the first is also the product of the shaping of that material from a single perspective. But as surely we do not want to exclude from a consideration of the diary the many writers who have followed Cummings's example, among them André Gide, Julien Green, and Max Frisch.[8]

We can get out of this dilemma, I think, by associating diaries edited for publication by their authors with diaries edited for publication by people other than their authors. When we speak of a diary, we

7. Hence, presumably, the questionable decision made by Kathleen Coburn to print the entries of Coleridge's notebooks not in the order in which they appear but in the closest approximation possible to the order in which they were written (*The Notebooks of Samuel Taylor Coleridge* [New York: Pantheon, 1957–73], vol. 1: xx–xxi).

Compare Harald Fricke's argument that aphorism books are characterized precisely by the possibility they offer of interchanging two adjacent aphorisms without altering the sense of either (Fricke, *Aphorismus* [Stuttgart: Metzger, 1984], p. 13).

8. Compare Frisch's "An den Leser": "the reader would do this book a great service if, declining to leaf through it as mood and chance dictated, he were to attend to its ordering sequence; the individual stones of a mosaic—and as such this book is at least intended—can hardly bear the responsibility on their own" (Frisch, *Tagebuch 1946–1949* [Frankfurt: Suhrkamp, 1981], p. 7)

always mean, implicitly, the whole of it.[9] When we read an abridged or altered version of a diary, as when we read an abridged or altered version of any text, we are reading at the same time the work of the writer and the work of the editor. The work of the editor is at once an obscuring and an interpretation of the work of the writer. Normally, we note principally the obscuring and try to read through it. Occasionally, when the editor interests us, we note also the interpretation, as in, say, Edmond Scherer's early edition of Amiel's diary, or Bliss Perry's *The Heart of Emerson's Journals*. Now Max Frisch the editor certainly interests us, and when we read *Tagebuch 1946–1949*, a selection from the work of Max Frisch the diarist, we will attend to the work of both diarist and editor. If, as in this case, we do not have access to the whole of which this is a part, we will not be able to do certain kinds of reading, just as we cannot do them with any of the many interesting editions of Amiel. In the end Frisch by Frisch, Green by Green, Gide by Gide are not essentially different than Boswell by Pottle, Emerson by Perry, Pepys by Braybrooke, all abridged and altered, but none the less clearly diaries for that, as perfection is surely no proper definitional criterion, here or anywhere else.

II

ALGERNON: Do you really keep a diary? I'd give anything to look at it. May I?

CECILY: Oh no. You see, it is simply a very young girl's record of her own thoughts and impressions, and consequently meant for publication. When it appears in volume form I hope you will order a copy.
OSCAR WILDE, *The Importance of Being Earnest*

Wilde's brilliance, perhaps, has obscured his good sense, and the myth Cecily's *mot* is aimed at has remained powerful. Let us consider it as manifested in Joel Porte's introduction to his excellent selection from Emerson's journal: "[Emerson] attempted to inscribe his soul in

---

9. It follows that for certain purposes we cannot judge a diary till its author is dead, since only then do we have a complete text. In this respect as in others a diary seems not so much a literary work as a literary *corpus*.

pages reserved for his eyes alone."[10] This is demonstrably false, and the evidence falsifying it abundant. In 1819, Emerson concludes an early volume of the journal by quoting "some remarks upon a few of its pages from the kindness of one who was persuaded to read them"; the kind reader was Emerson's aunt Mary Moody Emerson, whose journals Emerson read and remarked on in his turn. Bronson Alcott was told of Emerson's journals in 1838 and shown them casually after tea one April evening in 1839:

> Dwight left towards evening. After tea we conversed on style, my Conversations, the future. I looked over E's commonplace books.[11]

This was only fair play, since Emerson had read passages of Alcott's journal in 1836.[12] Margaret Fuller's journal records a more intimate scene:

> Waldo came into my room to read me what he has written in his journal about marriage, & we had a long talk. He listens with a soft wistful look to what I say, but is nowise convinced. It was late in a dark afternoon, the fine light in that red room always so rich, cast a beautiful light upon him, as he read and talked. *Since* I have found in his journal two sentences that represent the two sides of his thought . . . I shall write to him about it.[13]

Now Porte *knows* all this—no expert reader of Emerson's journals can be ignorant of it—yet he writes of a characterization of them that denies his knowledge. Emerson himself wrote in the book he so casually displayed that

> every young person writes a journal into which when the hours of prayer & penitence arrive he puts his soul. The pages which he has written in the rapt moods are to him burning & fragrant. He reads them on his knees by midnight & by the morning star he wets them.[14]

10. *Emerson in his Journals* (Cambridge, Massachusetts: Harvard University Press, 1982), p. v.

11. Odell Shepard, ed., *The Journals of Bronson Alcott* (Boston: Little, Brown, 1938), pp. 101 and 126.

12. William Gilman, et al., eds., *The Journals and Miscellaneous Notebooks of Ralph Waldo Emerson* (Cambridge, Massachusetts: Harvard University Press, 1960– 1982), 16 vols., V: 167–70. Subsequent citations will be identified in the text by JMN plus the volume and page number.

13. Belle Gale Chevigny, *Margaret Fuller: The Woman and the Myth* (Old Westbury, New York: Feminist Press, 1976), pp. 129–30.

14. JMN VIII: 123–24. The passage is followed by a merciless account of what is likely to happen when the young person finally resolves to show the cherished text to his dearest friend; the friend responds casually, even coldly, because, after all, the writing is simply not very good.

Not even one's *own* practice, it seems, can help here. We should begin by noting the myth of the diary as a secret text, since its hold over us is very great.

In fact the notion that diaries are necessarily private is simply false. If we wish to know whether a given diary was private, in the only *concrete* sense of private—that is, read or not read by readers other than the author—we have no choice but to find out. Having found out, we can see a given diarist's habits of secrecy and revelation in the context of a more general vision of the diarist or diaristic culture. New England Transcendentalists, we see, passed their diaries around as scholars pass around drafts of essays. New England Puritans who kept diaries of spiritual experiences seem not to have passsed them around to their contemporaries, but were used to reading them in the lives of their ancestors, and were injoined to preserve them for the use of their biographers and the edification of their descendants. Some diarists of course neither read other diaries nor reveal their own, though few, presumably, take the step necessary to keeping them private *in aeternum*, that namely of destroying them. Thus Samuel Pepys kept his diary in shorthand, sank certain erotic episodes still deeper into obscurity by recording them in a macaronic mixture of Spanish with English, French, Dutch, Italian, Latin, and Greek, and showed his diary to no one. *There*, one would say, we have a secret diary— indeed with a sort of split-level secrecy, dividing secrets from secrets by the firmament of language.[15] But then Pepys's best editors tell us that

> the care that Pepys took to ensure that the manuscript should seem clean and shapely, together with his pride in it and his pains to ensure its preservation in the library which he bequeathed for the use of future scholars, must mean that he intended it to have some of the qualities of a printed book . . . the volumes, after admission to his library, were kept (like the rest of the books) in locked presses, but the title "Journal" (discernible through the glazed doors) was printed on the spines, and

15. Pepys, *Diary*, Robert Latham and William Matthews, eds. (Berkeley: University of California Press, 1970–83), 1: lxi.

Split-level secrecy is fairly common. Cotton Mather uses Latin to recount ecstatic visions and episodes of his wife's madness, Michael Wigglesworth to discuss masturbation; E. T. A. Hoffmann uses Greek characters and various pictorial signs for his accounts of his beloved Kaetchen (Rosenwald, "Cotton Mather as Diarist," *Prospects* 8: pp. 144 and 151; Wigglesworth, *Diary*, Edmund Morgan, ed. (*Publications of the Colonial Society of Massachusetts* 35, 311–444, New York: Harper and Row, 1965); Hoffmann in Hocke, *Das Europaeische Tagebuch*, pp. 681–87).

the entries in his catalogues of 1693 and 1700 plainly recorded them several times (as "My own Diary," "Diary—Mr. Pepys's," etc.) in the longhand of an amanuensis.[16]

The question of audience and distribution is then to be settled *ad hoc*, not *a fortiori*, and the spectrum of behavior revealed by particular investigation is if nothing else far more interesting than that posited by the myth of necessary secrecy.

A solider distinction than that between secret and revealed is that between manuscript and book, though this distinction too has to be narrowed and qualified before it will do us much good. Before 1800 few daries were published *qua* diaries; many, however, were quoted extensively in biographies, and diarists must have considered their diaries to be, among other things, evidence and testimony.[17] But the independent publication of Evelyn's diary won respectful reviews in 1818, that of Pepys's considerable popularity in 1825, and that of Byron's (in Moore's *Memoirs*) European acclaim in 1830; by the 1830s, then, well-read diarists were surely considering the prospect of posthumous independent publication and, thus, inevitably thinking of their diaries as *books*. Barbellion's 1919 coup gave precedent for living diarists' entering the literary marketplace; over the course of the century the precedent has become almost an obligation, as diaries have followed autobiographies in becoming not so much books published as intimate guides to famous men and women as books published by men and women interested in becoming famous.[18]

Moreover, the opposition between manuscript and book is too crude; it presumes too wide a gap, too irreconcilable a difference. We know too well, perhaps, the difference between what we write on a scratch pad and the publications of a university press. Formerly, well-to-do men used the printing press as we use a xerox machine; into the gap between public and private creep, say, Samuel Sewall's numerous broadsides, or the hundred privately printed copies of the *Education* Henry Adams made to show his friends. But the practical distance

16. Pepys, *Diary*, 1: xlv and lxxi.

17. Boerner, *Tagebuch*, p. 18, writes that Voltaire in the *History of Louis XIV* was the first writer to use "contemporary journals for the illustration of historical context."

18. See Boerner, *Tagebuch*, pp. 51–59. Georges May, *De L'Autobiographie* (Paris: Presses Universitaires de France, 1979), p. 32, notes the novelty of Michel Leiris's having published his autobiography (*L'Age d'homme*) in 1946 at the age of 35: rather a first book than a last.

between even the unambiguous manuscript and the unambiguous book may not be very great. Let us suppose that over the course of his life Emerson showed his journal to fifty people. Thoreau published *A Week on the Concord and Merrimack Rivers* in 1849. One thousand copies were printed; two hundred ninety-four were sold. Where is the great gulf fixed between the distribution of a manuscript and the publication of a coterie book? Thoreau's famous comment on his own diaristic labors, "I was editor to a journal of no very wide circulation," takes on another meaning here. It reminds us not of the ironic difference between the journal that is a private diary and the journal that is a published magazine but of the underlying similarity between them that permits the joke: that both are texts, and both are distributed.

We must, then, set the diary within the local system of production and distribution, and not outside it; but that is not to say that we cannot within that system retain something of the concrete opposition between manuscript and book. In a sense, the diary is a manuscript not accidentally but essentially; if we think of a manuscript as a text in a fluid state, a diary is a manuscript by necessity. During the life of the diarist, the diary remains unfinished and open; something can always be added. Frisch publishes the past years of his diary, and we may class that text along with the diaries of Emerson and Thoreau; but we may also say that Frisch's diary is finally constituted only at Frisch's death and is until then essentially and not willfully incomplete and fluid, a text still within its author's power—though of course the same can be said of *Leaves of Grass*.

Appropriately, then, the diary is also a commodity within its author's power. Diarists distribute their texts to the readers they choose, novelists to the readers who can afford the publisher's price; diarists are craftsmen and novelists industrial workers; diarists are Luddites in the age of the mechanical reproducibility of works of art. It follows that diarists elect their audience,[19] and we can if we like speak of the diary as a text for the inner circle. But we will do well not to press the metaphor too hard; if the audience of the diary is an inner

19. Hence our sense, when we read a diary, that we are overhearing a secret. This sense results not from the nature of the material but from the conditions of distribution. We are, of course, in some sense not the intended audience of Boswell's *Life of Johnson*; but in publishing that work Boswell renounced any powerful claim that his intended audience need be his actual audience. Writers of diaries make no such renunciations, and their intentions regarding their audience can be realized in their practice. A diarist's intended audience is thus a far more concrete entity than a novelist's, and it is correspondingly clearer that we do not belong to it.

circle, the audience for a novel an outer circle, where as geometers are we to locate the audience of a letter? Nor ought we to presume that the audience of a particular diarist will realize some tendentious notion of intimacy; rather we can learn something about intimacy in its large sense by attending to what diaries tell us about it in its narrow sense. What we can presume is that the diarist creates not only a diary but an audience, and that we are bound to investigate both creations, translating the distinctions between private and public, intimate and distant, esoteric and exoteric, from the language of myth to the language of history.

III

The child is sincere, and the man when he is alone, if he be not a writer, but on the entrance of the second person hypocrisy begins.   EMERSON

I fear one lies more to one's self than to any one else.
                                                                          BYRON

Let us consider this passage from Michele Leleu's *Les Journaux intimes:*

Emerson clearly attests his lack of emotion (*inémotivité*) in his own self-description: "Ungenerous & selfish, cautious & cold, I yet wish to be romantic. Have not sufficient feeling to speak a natural hearty welcome to a friend or stranger . . . [this] is a true picture of a barren & desolate soul."[20]

Leleu is interested in Emerson's character—she is in fact a characterologist, and her book has the imprimatur of arch-characterologist René Le Senne—and to describe it, or rather as a piece of evidence regarding it, she confidently cites a passage of self-characterization taken from his journal.

This is a risky thing to do. Emerson's early journals are best described as deliberately unsystematic commonplace books, and as we read them we are continually conscious of the *literary* quality of what

20. Leleu, *Les Journaux intimes*, p. 189.

is written there, in such passages of self-characterization no less than in essays on the drama and on slavery. Behind the sentence Leleu quotes lies the literary tradition of the character from Bishop Hall and Samuel Butler to La Rochefoucauld and La Bruyère; and knowing this, we distrust her use of it. The interesting point, however, is that Leleu, like Porte, *knows* all this; she has noted the propensity of "phlegmatics" to use diaries as commonplace books on the page preceding the passage under discussion. It is not enough, then, to refute the individual error; what we have here is not a naive reader caught in a contradiction but an expert reader possessed by a myth. But though the myth of the private diary can be refuted by an appeal to fact, the myth of the veridical diary cannot be; it is founded irremovably because it is founded upon a void, founded not on an error of fact but on truths we hold to be self-evident.

Accordingly, George Gusdorf's classic account of that belief begins by identifying the powerful intuitions on which it rests.[21] The first of these is a belief about the self: that there exists within each of us a self independent of our consciousness of it. The second is a belief about perception: that the inward self is transparent to introspection. Setting out from these two positions, diarists may well feel that if they can only resist the contemptible temptation to dissemble, then the truth will come of itself, the fixed and immanent self be gradually revealed to candid introspection. This is Marie Bashkirtseff's confident account of the intoxicating prospect:

> I am entirely sincere. If this book isn't the *exact, absolute,* and *strict* truth it has no reason for being. Not only do I always say what I think— not for one instant have I ever dreamed of concealing what might seem laughable or discreditable in me. Anyway, I think too well of myself to want to censor me. So you may be certain, kind readers, that I shall present myself in these pages *in toto*. (43–44)

Gusdorf's refutation of this position proceeds along two lines. First, on grounds of principle: it simply cannot be the case that the self is distinct from our analysis of it and prior to it. In particular, it cannot be distinct from the very faculty and process of introspection intended to reveal it: "as Comte remarked, the original sin of introspec-

---

21. Gusdorf, *La Découverte de soi* (Paris: Presses Universitaires de France, 1948), pp. 26–88: "L'Attitude d'immanence," and especially pp. 69–77: "L'Échec du journal intime." Subsequent quotations from the book will be identified by page number in the text.

tion is that the seeing modifies the thing seen" (64). But our trust in introspection and our belief in the independent existence of our inward self are not analytical; they are intuitional and *feel* empirical. Gusdorf's most striking refutation of them is accordingly through testimony rather than through argument, in particular through testimony offered by the diarists for whom that trust and that belief have been central articles of faith.

Typically diarists follow two routes, which we may, following Gusdorf, call objective and subjective. The objective diarist seeks for the self in its daily manifestations: its actions, thoughts, and feelings. This choice leads inevitably to several impassable obstacles. The calendrical form comes to seem a distortion, forcing the diarist to create numinous events for boring days. The calendar is in any case too widely spaced a grid. So much slips through; a full account is impossible. A book of hours rather than of days, perhaps? Or a diary kept from minute to minute? "But no—the paper wouldn't have enough room," writes Julien Green. "And then, how to retrace the thread of thoughts so numerous and so rapid? As well try to retrace the flight of a flock of sparrows" (48).[22]

But perhaps this impossible task is not necessary. Perhaps diarists can find the self by attending only to what is genuinely important, by responding not to the calendar but to the rhythms of their own lives, by giving every event its proper treatment and amplitude. Perhaps, but eventually this approach too meets impassable obstacles. The first is the feeling, not specific to the moment but endemic to the enterprise, of having botched the job:

> Is it possible to keep a journal that gives even an approximately accurate idea of its author? I'm coming to doubt it. How am I to situate myself every day at the viewpoint that will give the right perspective? Necessarily we make frequent mistakes—give this matter an exaggerated importance, neglect another that will trouble us till death. We are too close to the landscape to distinguish foreground from background; we are in the middle of the landscape we want to paint, and our drawing is incorrect. (Green *apud* Gusdorf 51)

The second is that within the idea of selection lurks an assumption making nonsense of the entire enterprise. To select, to assess prop-

22. Later, Green finds the diarist's death sentence in Stevenson's essay on Whitman: "there are not words enough in all Shakespeare to express the merest fraction of a man's experience in an hour" (Green, *Journal 1928–1934* [Paris: Plon, 1938]), p. 87.

Is he not perhaps describing a contrast between genres, between cultures, between centuries?

We cannot really know; but we can at least finesse the problem. We can compare Boswell not with those diarists who make the comparison most striking but with those allotted him by the accidents of place and time, with his diaristic contemporaries and colleagues and countrymen.[24] We can look at his diary in light of the diaristic precepts he in fact thought pertinent to it, notably Samuel Johnson's,[25] just as graphologists studying a writer's hand insist on knowing the system by which the writer was taught. We can also compare him with the diarists he actually read, though here as almost everywhere the pattern of influences radically differs from that linking artists in other genres with one another, since novelists, say, read their major predecessors, while diarists cannot—Pepys is in some obvious way Boswell's natural father, but neither Boswell nor any other eighteenth-century diarist could ever have read him.

We need, that is, Boswell's diaristic ancestors, colleagues, and teachers if we are to know whether what Auden admires in Boswell is Boswell's or his culture's—or, more precisely, to get a sense of the mix in Boswell between tradition and the individual talent and to learn something about the *system* of talents within which Boswell's should be conceived. Like a phonetic element, a trait of style taken as evidence of a trait of character has to be read as part of a language.

Or more generally: the diary's importance as testimony to character lies in its status as a continuous record of comparable gestures. It is a series of entries; *qua* entries, they are comparable, and what they have in common constitutes a system of habits, a *modus operandi*. The *modus operandi* is instructively like handwriting. Like handwriting it expresses rather than describes the writer; like handwriting it can reliably distinguish one individual from another; and like handwriting it can be read as evidence not only of identity but also of character, by a reader knowing the conventions within which the writer operates.

But of course making a diary offers more expressive room than does writing a word. For one thing, the one includes the other,—and that

24. See as examples of this sort of practice Rosenwald, "Cotton Mather as Diarist," and Fothergill's comparison of Boswell with Dudley Ryder and William Windham (*Private Chronicles* [London: Oxford University Press, 1974], pp. 128–51: "Ego and Ideal").

25. Fothergill, *Private Chronicles*, pp. 25.

physical fact may remind us, in considering a diarist's *modus operandi*, to take into account not only the words but also their incarnation and format: the sort of book a diarist buys or makes to write in, and what it costs; how a volume of the diary is presented *qua* volume, what span of time it characteristically includes, whether it is given a formal beginning or ending; whether the text is immaculate or scribbled over with revisions; whether the page is exploited as a unit of organization; where dates are placed relative to the entries they govern; what non-verbal marks accompany the words.[26]

And the transcribed words themselves? We will want to identify norms and exceptions at every level of organization. We will want to note such matters as how long the average entry is, and how frequently and regularly entries are made; which subjects are treated at length, which in passing, which not at all; how entries are organized, whether by order of association or order of occurrence or order of exposition; what use is made of first- and second-person pronouns; which areas of the entry are habitual and which free—Pepys's marvelous improvisation so often tapers comfortably off into the formulaic "and so to bed"; how sentences are punctuated and words capitalized. As we identify each pattern we will be able to identify the anomalies clustered around it and ideally we will conclude this part of our study with a description not of habits only but of habits and singularities, habits and epiphanies. Gertrude Stein gives the best account of the process:

> I then began again to think about the bottom nature in people, I began to get enormously interested in hearing how everybody said the same thing over and over again with infinite variations but over and over again until finally if you listened with great intensity you could hear it rise and fall and tell all that that there was inside them, not so much by the actual words they said or the thoughts they had but the movement of their thoughts and words endlessly the same and endlessly different.[27]

But there is of course a further step. The diarist's *modus operandi* can be—must be—described as static, but the diary is kept in time.

---

26. In an early volume of Emerson's journal, an exhortation to diligence concludes, verbally: "Cast off your burden of apologies and compliances which retard your steps, and flee after them lest they reach your Lord and enter in before you and the door be shut.–" But the dash, the editors tell us, "has been extended into an open-mouthed snake's head with sharp fangs" (JMN II: 113).

27. Stein, "The Gradual Making of the Making of Americans," in Carl Van Vechten, ed., *Selected Writings of Gertrude Stein* (New York: Random House, 1946), p. 243.

Having described the *modus operandi* as it first becomes recognizable for us, we then must note how it changes—and at *every* level of organization, for it is as true from the diachronic perspective as from the synchronic that a set of habits is a way of being, and even the slightest modification registers a considerable tremor. Cotton Mather, some years after his wife's death from illness and the "miscarriage" of his "particular faith" that she would recover, gives up keeping a selective diary oriented precisely to the recording of such prophetic intuition and begins to keep an exhaustive diary of resolutions for good deeds— gives up, that is, both the experience that had misled him and the form oriented to its presentation, for an experience and form humbler in ambition and more manageable in execution. Some diaries of course retain their initial habits to the end, among them Pepys's; but that marvelous stability is itself testimony. The result is the same. A study of the *modus operandi* in stasis reveals the shape of a character, a study of it in motion the contours of a life.

All this may seem a timid refusal of a reliable access to obvious truth, and we may long for Leleu's unselfconscious assurance. But the longest way round is the shortest way home. We may justify our circumspection theoretically, by reference, say, to Austin's *How To Do Things With Words:*

> Once we realize that what we have to study is *not* the sentence but the issuing of an utterance in a speech situation, there can hardly be any longer a possibility of not seeing that stating is performing an act.[28]

But we may also justify it, and more powerfully, on the grounds of our common experience, as poker players, used car buyers, jury members, friends, and lovers. Stating is indeed "performing an act," whether by "act" we mean action or simulation. We need not accept our friends' sincerest self-assessments as truth; on the other hand, we know how our coolest antagonists' most adroit deception can reveal their inward parts and how much we give away of ourselves in our best attempts at concealment. The art of reading diaries as revelations of selves is the art we bring to making sense of other people in daily life.[29]

28. J. L. Austin, *How To Do Things With Words* (Cambridge, Massachusetts: Harvard University Press, 1962), p. 138.

29. Philippe Lejeune notes of autobiography that in it referential *accuracy* "is not critically important. It is essential in autobiography that the referential contract be *made,* and that it be *kept;* but . . . it may, by the reader's criteria, be kept *badly* without the text's diminishing thereby in referential value" (*Le Pacte autobiographique,* pp. 36–37).

IV

I should like to come back, after a year or two, & find that
[my diary] had sorted itself & refined itself & coalesced, as
such deposits so mysteriously do, into a mould, transparent
enough to reflect the light of our life, & yet steady, tranquil
composed with the aloofness of a work of art.

VIRGINIA WOOLF, April 20, 1919

We now come to the question of the diary's art and immediately
encounter the myth of the diary's artlessness. This myth like the
others is entangled in our intellectual practice; like them it can be
analyzed into its component tenets, and these scrutinized and im-
proved or replaced.

What exactly might "artlessness" mean? First, and most precisely,
it might mean the quality of a quickly and casually produced first
draft; it would be predicated of diaries in the belief that they are in
fact quickly and casually produced, and if so used would lead to
nothing worse than a harmless half-truth. It is probably true that on
the average diaries are less extensively reworked than are most classic
works of art, and in particular true that many writers' diaries, such as
Scott's, and Byron's, are less extensively reworked than their poems
and novels. But though some diarists do not revise their entries, some
do; and they are no less diarists for that. Pepys's diary gives an extraordinary impression of spontaneity and immediacy, and we count this
accomplishment a natural consequence of quick writing on recent
events; but Pepys is with the revisers. The text we call his diary was
surely not his first draft, and may on occasion have been his fifth; the
entries composing his vivid account of the Fire of London were pol-
ished to a single narrative in a single process of composition, several
weeks after the fire was over. Boswell took similar pains with his
celebrated account of the seduction of Louisa; Emerson rewrote the
journal of his travels in Italy while sitting in a ship bound for Boston.
To this spectrum of behavior the notion of the casually produced diary
is a very imperfect guide.

More often, however, "artlessness" is used to distinguish not between degrees of finish but between inexorably opposed and sundered antitheses: between "art" and "nature," that is, between a
well-wrought urn and some mode of spontaneous utterance wholly
unshaped by convention. The convenience and power of the opposi-

tion win over even the expert; thus William Matthews, whose brilliant edition of Pepys's diary is one source of the argument in the previous paragraph, writes that

> it is our habit when reading diaries to regard them as products of nature rather than of art. And in most cases the preconception is valid. Diaries *en masse* might well be regarded as natural products, and their commonly lumpish matters and styles witness the artlessness of their writers.[30]

To assert that journal accounts are governed only by the uncontaminated expressive impulses of the writer is false because it is impossible. All our utterances are mediated through our sophisticated or imperfect sense of some public, externally given form: refusing an invitation, summarizing a newspaper story, alluding to a sexual conquest. If "artlessness" means absolute freedom from convention it describes nothing. The things it is predicated of exhibit not "artlessness" but artistic incompetence, and the majority of diaries, like the majority of novels, bore the reader not because they are the products of nature but because they are the products of bad art.

How then can we describe the diarist's art? First, by acknowledging that it is in fact two arts: the art of the entry and the art of the diary as a whole.

Describing the art of the entry presents no theoretical problem, only a practical one: our general ignorance regarding the small forms of literature. Our sense of literary writing is macroscopic; it is more attentive to large forms than to small, the forms of lyric poetry excepted. We know little about the small discursive forms: the aphorism, the apothegm, the proverb, the bon mot, the *Spruch,* the *sententia,* the maxim, the reflection. We know little about the small narrative forms, the many varieties of anecdote. We know little about the small meditative forms. We know still less about the various forms to which a study of the entry impels us but for which we have no convenient names: the numerous varieties of ecphrasis, of edifying quotation, of vignette.[31]

What might we gain if we did know? Let us briefly consider the

30. Pepys, *Diary,* 1: cxi.

31. Some exceptions: on the whole subject, André Jolles, *Einfache Formen* (Halle: Niemeyer, 1930), also the discussion of Jolles in Ducrot and Todorov, *Dictionnaire encyclopédique,* pp. 200–201; on the aphorism see Gerhard Neumann, ed., *Der Aphorismus* (Darmstadt: Wissenschaftliche Buchgesellschaft, 1976; Wege der Forschung 356) and Fricke, *Aphorismus;* on the anecdote see Heinz Grothe, *Anekdote* (Stuttgart: Metzger, 1984); on the meditation see Louis Martz, *The Poetry of Meditation* (New Haven: Yale University Press, 1954).

great Puritan diarist Samuel Sewall. Sewall's best entries are clearly anecdotes rather than devotions, but "anecdotes" is only a rough description of them. To define their particular quality we would look at their available analogues: the anecdotal material in diaries like Sewall's, in almanacs and newspapers, in court records and on gravestones, in histories like Cotton Mather's *Magnalia Christi Americana* and records of strange happenings like Increase Mather's *Essay for the Recording of Illustrious Providences*. We would learn from this investigation that a Puritan anecdote is characteristically oriented toward an edifying punch line. Sewall's, however, are not, are more theatrical, because they present not one speaker in authority but two in conflict; that characterization would help us to make sense of the innovative and generous air of the debates he records between himself as suitor and the demurring ladies he courted. [32]

Describing the art of the diary as a whole presents both a practical problem and a theoretical one. The practical problem is similar to that just discussed: an ignorance of many of the neighboring forms. The large forms most similar to diaries are not only novels and autobiographies but also those forms which, like the diary, are large forms built of small: commonplace books, letter books, books of table talk, aphorism books, collections of jokes. [33]

The theoretical problem is more difficult. We have learned in the last century to see autobiography as a literary genre by attending not to the intractable givens of the author's life but to the plastic power of the author's word. Let authors order their lives into a *single* narrative, regard them from a *single* perspective, and we can read the narratives as art. But diarists write from as many perspectives as they make entries, and though they control each entry, it seems clear that they do not control the lifelong sequence of them. From a single perspective a writer can make a beginning and an ending: two-thirds of any literary form. But diarists cannot, or at least generally do not. Sometimes they produce a beginning, a deliberately initiatory entry; sometimes they do not, letting their diaries grow imperceptibly from scraps of paper or datebooks. Some make an ending: Cesare Pavese and Benjamin Haydon, who were about to commit suicide, and Pepys, who feared he was going blind. But most just *stop*—through

---

32. See further on this my "Sewall's *Diary* and the Margins of Puritan Literature," *American Literature* 58: 3, October 1986, pp. 325–41.

33. Two exceptions: on books of table talk see F. P. Wilson, "Table-Talk," *Huntington Library Quarterly* 4: 1940, pp. 27–46; on commonplace books see Ruth Mohl, *John Milton and his Commonplace Book* (New York: Ungar, 1969), pp. 11–30.

death, through loss of interest, through change of character or circumstances, through weakness—and Barbellion's gloomy prayer is most
often offered in vain:

> Day after day I sit in the theatre of my own life and watch the drama of my
> own history proceeding to its close. Pray God the curtain falls at the right
> moment lest the play drag on into some long and tedious anticlimax.[34]

Such seems to me a fair account of the strongest argument against
seeing the diary as a work of literature. It rests on two beliefs: that
diaries as wholes are in some way the work of chance rather than
design, and that works of chance are not works of art. Let us consider
both in turn.

To consider the first we shall have to look at diarists' actual behavior as readers and shapers of their texts. We find, as by now we may
expect to find, that is distributed evenly along a wide spectrum. Some
diarists, like Virginia Woolf, are at moments attentive readers of the
whole of their past diaristic creation and shape their future diaries in
response to the patterns that their reading has revealed.

> I got out this diary, & read as one always does read one's own writing,
> with a kind of guilty intensity. . . . there looms ahead of me the shadow
> of some kind of form which a diary might attain to. . . . What sort of
> diary should I like mine to be? Something loose knit, & yet not slovenly,
> so elastic that it will embrace anything, solemn, slight or beautiful that
> comes into my mind. I should like it to resemble some deep old desk, or
> capacious hold-all, in which one flings a mass of odds & ends without
> looking them through. . . . The main requisite, I think on re-reading
> my old volumes, is not to play the part of censor, but to write as the
> mood comes or of anything whatever; since I was curious to find how I
> went for things put in haphazard, & found the significance to lie where I
> never saw it at the time. But looseness quickly becomes slovenly. A
> little effort is needed to face a character or an incident which needs to be
> recorded. Nor can one let the pen write without guidance; for fear of
> becoming slack & untidy.[35]

Some, like Emerson and Thoreau, draw extensively on their journals
for the material of lectures and books; they are assiduous readers of
their texts, but seem conscious of them more as aggregates than as

---

34. *Apud* Fothergill, *Private Chronicles*, p. 169. Hence the practical and reason-
able distinction between a journal and a diary: a journal, for example Montaigne's
Journal de voyage en Italie, can have an ending because it is about a terminable and
foreseeably terminable *action;* a diary cannot, because it is about a *life.*

35. Anne Olivier Bell, ed., *The Diary of Virginia Woolf* (New York: Harcourt Brace
Jovanovich, 1977–), 1: 266 (April 20, 1919).

wholes. Some, like Scott, as they write one entry see only the entry they wrote the day before, and respond to local juxtapositions but not to large patterns. Some, like Pepys, seem seldom to look back at all;[36] and some, like Byron, swear not to.

> This journal is a relief. When I am tired—as I generally am—out comes this, and down goes everything. But I can't read it over; and God knows what contradictions it may contain.[37]

We cannot then presume that diaries as wholes are composed at random; diarists' relations to their diaries present a wide spectrum of varying degrees of control and awareness, and in studying any individual diarist we will need to ascertain where in that spectrum the diarist is to be found. But the spectrum is bounded. Diarists do not rewrite the entries of the distant past, nor can they predict even the immediate future, cannot foresee the deaths and wars and illnesses and maturations by which their lives and diaries will be modified. Each day they have a new chance at writing the perfect entry, the one exact culmination of all its predecessors; but their memories of those predecessors are inevitably faulty, their readings of them inevitably sporadic—what diarist could keep faithful watch over a constantly growing accumulation of many thousands of pages?[38]

How then do we read a diary as a whole? First, of course, we can read the diary as we read any author's collected works; everything said of the diary in the previous paragraph can be said of any literary *corpus*. But can we read a diary as a *single* literary work? We can, I think if we look briefly at the unexamined opposite; what do we mean by determinacy? Not, surely, that every word on the literary page is the optimal product of concluded deliberation; as Valéry has told us, poems are not finished, only abandoned. But it is over the words on the page that the author's control is surest. Over the field of literary

36. This is probably characteristic of diarists who write in shorthand, which facilitates recording but encumbers reading—that, as much as its secrecy, is its distinguishing trait as a notation.

37. *Apud* Fothergill, *Private Chronicles*, p. 57.

38. No study of the diary comments in *literary* terms on the fact that so many of the classic texts are so long (though for some disgruntled, insightfully practical comments see Alain Girard, "Le journal intime, un nouveau genre litteraire?" in *Cahiers de l'Association Internationale des Etudes Francaises* 17: 105). Pepys's diary in its most complete edition fills nine volumes, Thoreau's fourteen, Emerson's sixteen; Amiel's, which has never been published in its entirety, totals some fifteen thousand pages. Poe rejected from literary consideration any text not susceptible of being read in a single sitting; what are we to make of a text not susceptible of being read in a single year? In this respect too the literary diary seems similar not to a literary work but to a literary corpus.

possibility that precedes them it is clearly less so. An inkblot falls onto Rossini's manuscript page and suggests an arresting modulation. All poetry, we are told, is occasional, and all occasions contingent. The length of the book, its subject, the treatment of its subject, are affected by publishers' individual desires, by the taste of the public, by the rate of pay. The language itself is given, not elected. What follows the inscribing of words verges on anarchy. The typeface is what the printer has in stock; the line breaks and page breaks, the configuration of a page generally, are the product of chance. Critics are swayed by literary politics, readers by private fantasies. Operas are mediated through singers independent of composers, plays by actors independent of playwrights. The language itself will change, in part precisely in consequence of the work that its changes will alter. John Cage's *Imaginary Landscape no. 4,* a piece composed of what is played during a fixed period of time by twelve radios, each with one performer twirling its tuning-knob and one adjusting its volume, seems in this context not an aberration but a norm, and diaries in this context evidently vary from other artworks in degree rather than in kind, with diarists indeed retaining control over certain aspects of the transaction between writer and reader that novelists surrender.

The particular quantum of diaristic indeterminacy is not then a warning not to read diaries as literature but a hint about how to do it more intelligently. To read a diary we will want to find the local language for the play of chance and control. In the twentieth century, we may want John Cage's language:

> Observing the effects of the ego on my earlier works, I tried to remove it, by the use of *chance techniques,* in my later works. We discipline the ego because it alone stands between us and experience. I wanted to let the environment—or experience—into my music. . . .
>
> [My aim was] to make a musical composition the continuity of which [was] free of individual taste and memory (psychology) and also of the literature and "traditions" of the art. . . .
>
> What is the purpose of writing music? . . . an affirmation of life—not an attempt to bring order out of chaos nor to suggest improvements in creation, but simply a way of waking up to the very life we're living, which is so excellent once one gets one's mind and one's desires out of its way and lets it act of its own accord.[39]

39. Cage in R. C. Clark, "Total Control and Chance in Musics: A Philosophical Analysis," *Journal of Aesthetics and Art Criticism* 28: 357; Cage, *Silence* (Middletown, Connecticut: Wesleyan University Press, 1973), pp. 12 and 59.

We may, that is, want to distinguish invidiously between things as we order them and things as they are.[40] For the Romantics, we will want to think of Goethe's experiments in automatic writing and the image of the Aeolian harp, and of Eckermann's justification of the contradictory opinions reported in his *Conversations with Goethe* on the ground of a notion of wholeness. For Emerson and Nietzsche we will need the language of character and will: Nietzsche's remark that "if someone has a character, he will also have a set of experiences happening again and again," Emerson's that "the reason of the event is always latent in the life." For the Puritans we will need the notion that a life is not so much the work of human will as God's plot, or Pascal's remark that "every author has a meaning to which all his contradictory passages constitute a harmony or he has not meaning at all." All the various languages for the opposition between the self and the not-self can help us in reading the diary that is the product of both.

V

What are the results of these polemical investigations? We can state them most clearly as a series of topics to be considered in the study of individual diarists: how the text was made, how and to whom it was distributed, how and from whom kept secret; how these practices fit within the larger patterns of production and distribution and secrecy characterizing the diarist's culture; the diarist's *modus operandi;* how the *modus operandi* fits within the diaristic context, that is, the diarists the diarist actually read, the local precepts regarding diary keeping, the diaries kept by the diarist's diaristic colleagues; how the *modus operandi* fits within the literary context, that is, the literary

---

40. See also Clark, "Total Control and Chance in Musics," and Leonard Meyer, "The End of the Renaissance," in *Music, The Arts, and Ideas* (Chicago: University of Chicago Press, 1967), pp. 68–84. Meyer calls Cage's sort of art "anti-teleological," meaning that it reflects not only a belief regarding the self's relation to the not-self but also a belief about the world comprising both: that it is a world of events and not of causal sequences. From that belief, he continues, we come quickly enough to a distrust of ordered sequence, not, as in Cage's account, because we distrust the *orderer*, but now because we distrust the *sequence*, with its suggestions of necessity, of determinateness, of one auditory event's seeming to cause or be caused by another. Cage's account is essentially psychological, and describes the condition of mind consonant with an interest in aleatoric music; Meyer's is essentially philosophical, and supplements Cage's by making good sense of the forms which that state of mind will yield, in particular its predilection for indistinct beginnings and inconclusive endings.

system of the diarist's culture; the evolution of the *modus operandi* over time, and the relationship of that evolution to the shape of a life; the aesthetic relationship between the entry, which the diarist controls, and the diary as a whole, which is at least partly the work of chance; the place of that relationship within the larger patterns of the culture, notably the local language for the play of control and chance that every diary considered necessarily permits us to witness and to experience. The following series of essays is an exploration of those topics in connection with the extraordinary journals of Ralph Waldo Emerson.

II

From Commonplace Book to Journal

The voyage of the best ship is a zigzag line of a hundred tacks.

"Self-Reliance"

Although temperamentally given to epiphanies, Emerson found his diaristic form by fits and starts. Accordingly, the present account of that process follows a zigzag line. The first and longest section gives an account of the beginning and ending of the Wideworld series, comprising the first thirteen volumes of the journal; it describes the form of those volumes as a product of the normative model of the commonplace book expounded by John Locke and the subversive influence of the spiritual journal kept by Mary Moody Emerson, and presents Emerson's altering of that form as a denial, not of the influence, but of the normative authority, of the Lockean model. The second section narrates two brief episodes of diaristic apostasy: the atrophy of the journal during Emerson's ministry, and its metamorphosis into a travel book during his first trip to Europe. It presents these episodes as a story of how in the absence of the Lockean authority Emerson yielded to certain temptations leading him astray from the development of a genuinely Emersonian journal, suggesting at the same time that precisely this yielding to temptation made possible Emerson's conscious achievement, just after his return from Europe, of the form he had just been straying from. The last section presents the first of Emerson's mature journals as a form by which the conflicting influences bearing on the journal are consciously harmonized; it pays particular attention to Emerson's development of a new system of indexing, taking this as a formal development necessary to Emerson's writing of a journal harmonizing such diverse influences and also expressive of Emerson's consciousness that such was the journal he was now and henceforth to keep.[1]

Authority and Rebellion

At the beginning of Wideworld 1, the first volume of Emerson's journal, we find a declaration of genre:

> these pages are intended at this their commencement . . . for all the various purposes & utility real or imaginary which are usually comprehended under that comprehensive title *Common Place book*. (JMN I: 3–4)

At the end of Wideworld I, we find an indication of sub-genre: an index of the topics the volume covers arranged according to the particular method of keeping a commonplace book devised by John Locke. We know that Emerson's elder brother Edward had a copy of Locke's method. We may then posit Locke's method as a model for Emerson's enterprise.[2]

No literary historian could ask for an apter or more suggestive model; a general rebellion against Locke was of course one of the creative movements by which New England Transcendentalism came into being,[3] and as we see Emerson choose Locke as his diaristic authority, we inevitably and to some extent rightly feel that we can already define Emerson's career as a diarist as a rebellion against the model he begins with. But even literary rebellions borrow much of

1. On the early journals see Ralph LaRosa, "Emerson's Search for Literary Form: The Early Journals" (*Modern Philology* 69:25–35), which despite its title concerns not the form of the journals but the form of the sentences they contain, and also Evelyn Barish Greensberger, "The Phoenix on the Wall: Consciousness in Emerson's Early and Late Journals" (*American Transcendental Quarterly* 21: 45–56).

2. "Posit," because though Wideworld I was written in 1820, Edward's copy of Locke's method not published until 1821. The JMN editors propose two hypotheses: that Emerson had access to an earlier edition of the method, or that he added the index in 1821. Neither hypothesis diminishes the heuristic value of positing Locke's method as Emerson's model, though the latter forbids us to take it as his point of origin. The method was in any case in the air; my colleague David Ferry called my attention to Boswell's casual mention of Johnson's use of it for the *Rambler* (Boswell, *Life of Johnson* [New York: Modern Library, 1931], pp. 118–21).

3. See on this Cameron Thompson, "John Locke and New England Transcendentalism" (*New England Quarterly* 35: 1962, 435–57).

what they rebel against; and as we watch Emerson turn gradually away from the method Locke instituted, it will be good for us to keep in mind that the great Transcendentalist was only the great Empiricist's antagonist after being his disciple.

Locke's method describes both a particular sort of commonplace book and the program of activity necessary to produce it. The first step of the program is the drawing up of an index page; this comprises one hundred boxes in all, with each of twenty initial letters being allotted five boxes, and each of the five vowels by which the initial letters may be followed being allotted one box of the five. Then, having prepared the index page, the commonplacer sits down to read. When he comes across a passage worth transcribing, he makes a note of it. Later, his stint of reading done, he turns to the first pair of *empty* facing pages in the commonplace book, transcribes the passage, assigns it a subject heading, and enters the subject and page number in the appropriate slot on the index page. If, that is, he has filled pages two and three with material relating to miracles, pages four and five with material relating to skepticism, and then comes across more material on miracles, he enters it on page six, indicates the new page number under the old subject heading, and adds at the end of the earlier entry a note indicating the location of the later.

What are the implications of this method? Practical experience of it will teach us to feel the pressure imposed by the necessity of devising a subject heading for a passage directly upon entering it. Locke's method, that is, requires *rapid* classification; it implies that category inheres visibly in the passage itself, not in the use a writer may later make of it. Clearly, Locke's commonplacer lives in a world of sharply and evidently differentiated topics, and of passages clearly and inevitably belonging to them; nowhere does the method allow for the difficulty we may feel in assigning a passage to a topic, or for our pleasure in finding a passage belonging to several topics at once. Topics are immediately available and inherently appropriate for the passages we come across, pressing themselves on our passive notice much as do the sensory data of experience themselves in the Lockean epistemology.

But the real genius of Locke's method is its elimination of the circumstantial. Let us imagine an actual reading session. It is, say, Thanksgiving Day, cold and blustery; I am sick in bed, reading desultorily, and find myself skipping from C. S. Lewis's defense of miracles to Samuel Johnson's celebrated comparison of Pope with Dryden to a newspaper report of a murder. Perhaps my interest in this last passage has something to do with my experience of the previous passages, or with the weather, or with my state of health, or with the holiday on which I am reading. Perhaps, moreover, we may think it of some importance to see our choice of passages as reflecting who we are, where we find ourselves in a sequence of events, in a historical context. Locke clearly does not; his method cleverly and efficiently removes the detritus of historical or personal context clinging to the passages we dredge up and leaves them bright, clean, and isolated, isolated not only from us who found them, from the context in which they emerged as interesting, but also from one another—for never, never in a Lockean commonplace book will a *fait divers* face a justification of miracles. Entries are first purified of the circumstances of their discovery and then placed on a page in isolation, incapable of generating the serendipitous interest of accidental juxtaposition.

This is of course only as it should be: what better way to prevent that association of ideas that Locke identified as the great source of error? But there is another justification also. We imagine the serendipitous interest of accidental juxtaposition as a charm offered by a book to a reader; but Locke's commonplace book is not a book for a reader but an instrument for a writer. For why, after all, are we keeping a commonplace book in the first place? Primarily, it turns out, so that we can make use of it for public argument and public advancement:

> In all sorts of Learning . . . the Memory is the *Treasury or Storehouse*, but the Judgment the *Disposer*, which ranges in order whatever it hath drawn from the Memory. . . . For it would be to little Purpose to spend our Time in Reading of Books, if we could not apply what we read to our Use. . . .
>
> [These details of method] it's likely may seem Minute and Trivial, but without 'em great Things cannot subsist, and these being neglected cause very great Confusion both of Memory and Judgment, and that which above all Things is most to be valued, Loss of Time.
>
> Some who otherwise were Men of most extraordinary *Parts*, by the Neglect of these things have committed great Errors, which if they had been so happy as to have avoided, they would have been much more serviceable to the Learned World, and so consequently to Mankind.[4]

This is the argument of Jean Leclerc in the epistle introducing Locke's method. It evokes Benjamin Franklin; but it also bears an

4. From John Lock [sic], *A New Method of Making Common-Place-Books* (London: J. Greenwood, 1706), pp. i–ii and v.

uncanny resemblance to *Reader's Digest* exhortations to "increase your word-power," which are directed not to the delights of language but to the attainment of an executive vice-presidency, and it makes clear that Locke's method of keeping a commonplace book is among other things an instrument for *success*. It is intended not to cultivate reading but to govern it; it implies that reading, unless directed to "the Learned World, and so consequently to Mankind," is a dissipation and a temptation. Pure reading, desultory reading are made by it to seem a little sinful, and the faculty of memory, with its jumbled richness of impressions, is placed by it under the strict control of the judgment.

In many ways, Emerson does surprisingly well as a Lockean commonplacer. Each volume is dedicated to a topic. Locke had suggested keeping one commonplace book for moral philosophy, one for natural philosophy, one for "the *Science,* or *Knowledge* of *Signs*";[5] Emerson's early volumes seem an attempt to go Locke one better. The figures made much of in the early journals include such local images of public success as Webster and Channing and Everett. The topics made much of include "Greatness," "Pulpit Eloquence," "Fame," and "Improvement." Much of the other material suggests a similar concern by its style. It falls chiefly into two categories: justifications of Christian doctrine and essays in the style of the quarterlies. The first are evidently intended for the use of Emerson the minister; they articulate and defend comfortable doctrines. Of the essays something more should be said, because when we think of Emerson the essayist we think of the tradition running from Montaigne and Bacon through the English Romantics to Emerson's own two collections in the 1840s— that is, we think of a form one of whose charms is the impression it gives of a private voice speaking in public, of the spontaneous and idiosyncratic movement of thought that the Lockean commonplace book is intended to tame and discipline. But the essayistic portions of the early journals are not at all in that tradition; they evoke the *Spectator,* and more immediately the *Monthly Anthology* and the *North American Review* and their English and Scottish models, all of which Emerson read and celebrated.[6] They are, that is, arguments

5. Ibid., p. 10.
6. "You like the Edinburgh Reviews; by only reading one solid dissertation there, where the finest ideas are ornamented with the utmost polish and refinement of language you will feel some enthusiasm to turn your own steps into a *new* path of the field of belles lettres—" (Ralph L. Rusk, ed., *The Letters of Ralph Waldo Emerson* [New York: Columbia University Press, 1939; henceforth abbreviated as L], 6 vols., vol. I, p. 61).

laying down the law, in which an expert speaks to a public seeking either to be informed about subjects of which it is ignorant or instructed about issues concerning which it is in doubt.

In all these aspects the journals seem the ample storeroom of an edifying public speaker. A storeroom, however is arranged by category; Emerson's journals are arranged by time. And with the chronological ordering of dated entries returns all that Locke had so efficiently banished. Every *aperçu*, every extract, every passage that for Locke is a *thing* becomes for Emerson an *event*. Locke's sample commonplace book has a passage on the Ebionites, and that passage is simply raw material, classified for future use. Emerson's journal has an entry on slavery and then an entry on the Greeks, and those entries are events in a story set in time. Or, more precisely, they are *actions;* the temporal context they imply is not the calendar but their author's life, and the story they occur in is their author's story. Moreover, the juxtapositions Locke had so adroitly prevented are here made inevitable. Emerson writes first about slavery, later about divine omniscience, and in writing creates a *page* on which the two accounts of authority and submissiveness inevitably collide. The Lockean commonplace book portrays inexorably sundered categories, the Emersonian journal indissolubly linked facets. The Lockean commonplace book is a piece of work done by the writer, distinguishing one category from another; the Emersonian journal evokes the possibility of work to be done by the reader, the work of understanding that categories are initially distinguished only that they may ultimately efface before a perception of unity. "The whole fascination of life for Emerson," writes O. W. Firkins, "lay in the disclosure of identity in variety, that is, in the concurrence, the *running together,* of several distinct images or ideas."[7] The Lockean commonplace book inhibits that fascination, the Emerson commonplace book stimulates it.

To what force can we attribute Emerson's resistance to the Lockean model? The journal itself will suggest an answer. Its name and its

---

7. Firkins, *Ralph Waldo Emerson* (Boston: Houghton Mifflin, 1915), p. 237; appositely cited in Lawrence Buell, *Literary Transcendentalism* (Ithaca: Cornell University Press, 1973), p. 156.

The quotation book "Universe," the "Catalogue—of Books read from the date December 1819," and the College Theme Book, all contemporary with Wideworld 1, also are dated and arranged chronologically. They are in consequence pretty much unusable; what would Emerson do to find a particular quotation or book? So the preference for chronological order is stronger, at least in this case, than the preference for utility.

structure are derived from Locke; but its most prominent character is Emerson's remarkable aunt Mary Moody Emerson. It is she who is represented most often and at greatest length in her own words. She read his journals and he hers, each commenting on the other's in their correspondence. It is letters to and from her that the journal records, which is otherwise no letter book.[8] The JMN editors have chosen to exclude such of these as have been printed elsewhere, either in the earlier edition of the journal or in Rusk's edition of the letters. It is hard to fault a sixteen-volume edition for its exclusions, but these exclusions conceal the nature of Emerson's enterprise: Emerson was creating a *book,* one of the components of which was an excerpted version of his correspondence with his aunt, the *genius loci* of the Emersonian journal.[9]

Now Mary Moody Emerson's influence on Emerson's general intellectual development is no secret; every biographer takes cognizance of it, and in particular the influence of the aunt's journal on the nephew's general intellectual development has been intelligently explored by Phyllis Cole.[10] But as we deny that Emerson's writings live by their form, we have not as yet considered the obvious formal questions that relationship evokes. Mary Moody Emerson was the one strong diarist pertinent to Emerson's early diaristic development.[11] What sort of journal did she keep, and what would her gifted nephew have learned from it about the enterprise he was engaged upon?

8. In L I: 96, Rusk notes the difficulty of deciding whether a particular passage of Emerson's prose is "from a letter [to Mary Moody Emerson] or from a scrap of Emerson's journals."

9. The editors note that in Blotting Book Y "a further sheet, containing a letter to Mary Moody Emerson, was tipped with red sealing wax onto the left margin of the page numbered 5" (JMN III: 163); see also Emerson's remark, JMN V: 138, "I find an old letter to L[idian]. which may stand here." Surely these explicit cues suggest that Emerson put letters into the journals by deliberate choice.

10. Cole, "The Advantage of Loneliness: Mary Moody Emerson's Almanacks, 1802–1855," in Joel Porte, ed., *Emerson: Prospect and Retrospect* (Cambridge, Massachusetts: Harvard University Press, 1982, Harvard English Studies, vol. 10).

11. Emerson later read a good many other diarists, most of those diaries were written long before his aunt's: Samuel Johnson by 1827 (JMN VI: 65), Pepys by 1838 (JMN VI: 347), Bubb Dodington by 1841 (JMN VIII: 134), Emerson's great-grandfather Joseph Emerson of Malden on his 1847–48 trip to Europe (Rusk, *The Life of Ralph Waldo Emerson* (New York: Scribner's, 1949), p. 330), Evelyn by 1854 (JMN VI: 370), Varnhagen von Ense by 1863 (JMN VI: 349), Henry Crabbe Robinson some time after 1869 (JMN VI: 372). Pepys is the diarist one would like Emerson to have read early, as being an interesting antagonist; but the ideal lines of filiation for diarists and the actual ones seldom cross.

Mary Moody Emerson's journal was a descendant of the Puritan journal of spiritual experiences: the perfect antagonist for the Lockean commonplace book.[12] The commonplace book is a book of others, the Puritan journal is a book of the self. The commonplace book is a book of topics arranged in order of convenience, the journal a book of events arranged in order of occurrence. The commonplace book is directed to success in what Emerson's Puritan ancestors would have referred to as the particular calling: the writer's public, professional life in the world. The journal is directed to salvation, to success in what the Puritans would have referred to as the general calling: the writer's striving for a justified soul.[13]

If we posit the influence of Mary Moody Emerson as an antagonist to that of Locke, where in the battleground of the text can we see it manifested? Most obviously in the numerous self-reflective passages of the journal; but these require some discussion. They are not really in Mary Moody Emerson's vein; they are not occupied with the moral status of Emerson's soul. They never predominate in the journal, nor are they consistently more interesting than passages concerned with other topics. Emerson excels neither in self-deception nor in self-knowledge; he has his reserves and his rhetorical evasions, and in the talent of honesty Boswell and Pepys are his evident superiors. But neither do the self-reflective passages ever disappear; they are, if not predominant, at least ineradicable. We might say of them that just as the decision to date and juxtapose notations of lofty truths suggested something of Emerson's sense of the necessarily personal, temporal nature of those truths, so this decision to include notations regarding the self among those truths suggests something about Emerson's sense of the possibly lofty, public, almost impersonal nature of the

12. The account of the Puritan journal offered here is based on Rosenwald, "Cotton Mather as Diarist," pp. 131–33.

13. Mary Moody Emerson's early correspondence with her nephew is among other things a running critique of his lively interest in the variety of the world, that is, of his distressing *commitment* to his particular calling; it is thus an attack both on the ends and means of the Lockean commonplace book as this is aimed at furthering worldly success by means of judicious quotation from the accumulated stock of traditional wisdom: "Would to Providence your unfoldings might be [in solitude]—that it were not a wild & fruitless wish that you could be disunited from travelling with the souls of other men of living & breathing, reading & writing with one vital time-sated idea— *their opinions*" (JMN II: 381). Emerson's playful comment in a letter to his aunt expresses the same tension: "I made a journal as we went, and have not read it over myself, but apprehend it hath too many *jokes* to please you; it was written for a more terrestrial meridian" (L I: 115).

self. It is a commonplace book that Emerson is keeping; but he will find room in it for introspection and self-depiction, not counting these things unworthy of his lofty purpose.

The dedications and afterwords of the individual volumes suggest a similar resistance to the Lockean enterprise. Within the text are edifying essays; at its margins are the dedications and afterthoughts. These are characteristically personal, self-conscious, and entire. Certainly they are not profitable texts, nor are they inevitably adaptable to some larger public discourse. They are much occupied with the business of journalizing, and in being so occupied are at odds with the Lockean scheme, which is not set up to reflect upon itself.

But the rebellion is endemic to the journal as a whole. As we read, we feel the essayistic material as an antagonist to everything surrounding it: the personal reflections, the occasional aphorism or exclamation or anecdote or quotation, the epigraphs, the dedications, the closing reflections, the comic self-compliments ("Dum a dum, now, but the book *does* grow better" (JMN I: 127)), the impudent index categories like "Trash" and "Abortions" (JMN I: 93 and 122; see also JMN II: 256, 269, 285, and 312). Writing for use seems to alternate with writing for pleasure, and brilliant flourishes of quotations at the beginnings and endings of volumes frame dutiful essays within them. Sometimes the contrasts flourish at the center; one spectacular outbreak in Wideworld 6 offers in succession an essayistic passage on habit; a personal reflection; the statement that "there is a great difference whether the tortoise gathers h/im/er self within h/is/er shell hurt or unhurt", a reflection on the journal; a note on Marchand's sighting of Mowna Roa at a distance of one hundred fifty-nine miles; an essayistic passage on characteristics of the passions; the often-quoted, heavily cancelled "I have a nasty appetite which I will not gratify;" a further personal reflection; a note on Harrison Otis's "Prodigious display of Eloquence;" the statement "I love my wideworlds;" two edifying anecdotes of fifteenth-century Italian manners from Sismondi; and a notation that Emerson weighs 144 pounds (JMN I: 128–35).

We should note further of this extraordinary stretch of writing that only the essayistic passages of it get indexed: the passages on habit, on "Characteristics," on self, on history. The rest are simply *written*, not written for use, nor digested for the index. The Lockean commonplace book, of course, *exists* for its index; material not classified in the index is hardly material at all. The abundance of material in the

Emersonian journal not reflected in its Lockean index is a final, mute sign of a house divided.

Emerson's own language for the division is the Romantic discourse of diligence and indolence. He associates the Lockean enterprise with heroic diligence, the Moodyan resistance to that enterprise with indolence, with caprice, with "silliness," and with the self.

> —Now here again is another detached morsel intended to be merely the first lines of a long treatise upon fate & life, &c, but it is cropped in the bud by the fiend Caprice; and I must gallop away to some new topic which my fantastic Genius may suggest . . . (JMN I: 123)
>
> I have rambled far away from my original thought, still there is a loose unity which binds these reflections together and which leads me back to the dubious theme—myself . . . (JMN II: 111)
>
> My cardinal vice of intellectual dissipation—sinful strolling from book to book, from care to idleness, is my cardinal vice still; is a malady that belongs to the Chapter of Incurables. (JMN II: 332)[14]

This is familiar talk, but has distinct Emersonian colorings. In Keats's famous letter to Reynolds, "busyness" hardly has a fair shake and "indolence" has it all its own way.[15] This is partly because Keats himself, like Coleridge, did not need to fear the reproach "indolence" usually entails; both writers could celebrate indolence because neither was lazy. Emerson really was; he did "stroll" from book to book and from topic to topic. Thus he would dedicate each volume of the journal to a particular topic. The topics were various: the dead, imagination, the spirit of America, the future. But Emerson did not keep to them; given one subject, he inevitably wrote on another.[16] He was one of the most desultory readers and writers of all time, and he might plausibly worry that he was incapable of the sustained and directed effort the Lockean enterprise entailed. Nor was he, as we have already noted, inclined to give up on that enterprise; he wove it into the fabric of his journal. Later, of course, Emerson will write over his door the word whim. But for now, "the fiend caprice" is his

14. See also JMN II: 244–45, 302, 309, and 317–18.
15. See Lionel Trilling, ed., *The Selected Letters of John Keats*, (Garden City: Doubleday Anchor, 1951), pp. 122–25, and also Trilling's own comments on the issue in his introduction, pp. 21–23.
16. See in this context his account of his discomfort with the formal constraints of the individual volume itself: "this last effort of the pen seems to have been tortured out for the mere purpose of ending the book, and I really regret that the sixth widewold which boasts of several swelling paragraphs, should close its page with so heartless an oration" (JMN I: 157).

enemy, not his champion; the unity of the self is a *pis aller;* want of method is associated with blundering and selfish rebellion, and desultory reading with disease and vice. We might say that resolution and independence are in even battle.

Given such strains, it is no surprise that the balance cannot hold: in 1824, the Wideworld series ends. But the ending of the series is not a precisely defined event,[17] nor does it point clearly to a precisely definable motive on Emerson's part, so we shall have to look closely at what happens throughout the period of transition. Emerson himself says nothing about it at the time; but his very interesting comments on the matter fifteen years later suggest much about the nature of the change, associating it in particular with his rejection of the Lockean notion of topicality.

> I need hardly say to any one acquainted with my thoughts that I have no System. When I was quite young I fancied that by keeping a Manuscript Journal by me, over whose pages I wrote a list of the great topics of human study, as, *Religion, Poetry, Politics, Love,* &c in the course of a few years I should be able to complete a sort of Encyclopaedia containing the net value of all the definitions at which the world had yet arrived. But at the end of a couple of years my Cabinet Cyclopaedia though much enlarged was no nearer to a completeness than on its first day. Nay somehow the whole plan of it needed alteration nor did the following months promise any speedier term to it than the foregoing. At last I discovered that my curve was a parabola whose arcs would never meet, and came to acquiesce in the perception that although no diligence can rebuild the Universe in a model by the best accumulation or disposition of details, yet does the World reproduce itself in miniature in every event that transpires, so that all the laws of nature may be read in the smallest fact. So that the truth speaker may dismiss all solicitude as to the proportion & congruency of the aggregate of his thoughts so long as he is a faithful reporter of particular impressions. (JMN VII: 302–3)

As Emerson tells the story, the early journal seems purely a commonplace book, the individual volumes of it essentially topical collections, the overall goal the compilation of an encyclopedia. The goal proves unreachable, the circle of knowledge Emerson is seeking to enclose turns out to be an eternally open parabola. So Emerson sets

17. "Wideworld No XIII" is the last extant journal to bear the title. The next extant volume is numbered XV but untitled; reference is made in it to a volume numbered XIV, but it is not clear whether that volume was titled or not.

out on a different principle, striving not to build up the macrocosm but to record the microcosm, trusting that the "the World [does] reproduce itself in miniature in every event that transpires," that "every thought is a world,—is a theory of the whole" (JMN IV: 53).[18] This of course implies a much altered relation between the observer and the object. In the earlier model, the observer must strain for "proportion and congruency [in] the aggregate of his thoughts," that is, congruency of one intrinsically partial thought to another. But if each thought is a whole, proportion and congruency cease to be adequate standards; fidelity alone is an adequate standard, because the distinction is not between congruent and incongruent aggregates but between sincere and insincere impressions.

This is an imperfect description of the early journal, of course. It minimizes the tension the journal reflects, and in it Emerson the early diarist seems a more devout and diligent Lockean common-placer than he ever was, just as the new diarist seems much less of one than he was in fact to be. What has happened is not the elimina-tion of a predominant influence but an adjustment in the relation between that influence and the influence opposing it. It is not that the Lockean influence is gone; it is that it is no longer normative. Emer-son singles out topicality as if it constituted the whole of the Lockean program. It does not; but it is the thing Emerson gains freedom in giving up. Keeping to a topic is the thing Emerson cannot do, and in ending the Wideworld series he rejects the claim that he should. He remains a Lockean commonplacer; but Locke is now not his norma-tive model but one among his possibilities.

So revised, Emerson's account suggests how to make sense of the changes we note clustering around the last few Wideworld volumes. The dedications of the individual volumes shrink, then disappear in June of 1823. This is as it should be; the dedications are assertions of topic, titles of volumes in this individual cabinet cyclopedia, and the shrinkage in them presages the abandonment of the system they reflect. But the reflections on journalizing are more abundant: indices

18. See also further along this line L II: 441 and JMN IV: 322, and especially JMN VIII: 224: "Having once learned that in some one thing although externally small, greatness might be contained, so that in doing that, it was all one as if I had builded a world; I was thereby taught, that everything in nature should represent total nature; & that whatsoever thing did not represent to me the sea & sky, day & night, was something forbidden and wrong."

of the coming alteration in the nature of the enterprise. The celebrated self-portrait "Myself," written in 1824 (JMN II: 237–42), suggests the heightened self-consciousness one might expect to attend such an alteration.[19]

Around the same time, the essayistic passages of the journal get worse. Emerson's prose *in them* becomes only more turgid and strained, the sequence of argument from paragraph to paragraph more tenuous. And Emerson knows it; his derisive after-comments become more frequent and more biting. The dedication to Wideworld 11 concludes, "dead ere it reached its original idea. One more of my extensive family of still born trains" (JMN II: 146). After an essayistic passage on apathy (JMN II: 158) he writes "fine marble form! Would it might wake to life." This too is as it should be; for the essay of the quarterlies that Emerson is trying to write is essentially *contributory* to a "cabinet cyclopedia" and formally akin to an encyclopedia entry.

The essayistic passages are worse; but they are also differently conceived. This is an auspicious but complex symptom. In the earlier volumes Emerson is sometimes using the journal as a themebook, writing down, say, the partial but sequential passages of an essay on drama; and generally the individual essayistic passages feel essentially incomplete, imperfect components of an unrealized perfect particular whole. Against this stands in the early journals all the other material, which feels by contrast irresponsibly autonomous, as if a piece of a mosaic offered itself as a freestanding sculpture. But now the essayistic material itself changes; now Emerson is producing passages in some sense complete within themselves. We can imagine them as parts of essays, but are not compelled to imagine them as parts at all, nor to imagine them as parts of one essay only. This is an auspicious symptom as it looks towards the nature of Emerson's mature essays, whose excitement arises from the juxtaposition of wholes, not from the fusing of parts; but it is still more auspicious as it looks towards the mature journal, which is precisely the record kept by "a faithful reporter of particular impressions," indifferent to "the proportion &

19. Mary Moody Emerson writes to Emerson on April 13, 1824, "it was ingeniously done to write so well on my old almanacks" (JMN I: 373). The letter she is responding to is lost, but was presumably written during the period we are now discussing, and perhaps Emerson's articulate response to his aunt's diaries was part of his rethinking his own.

congruency of his thoughts" as these awkward essayistic fragments are indifferent and incongruent to one another.[20]

So described, the essayistic passages seem like the products of Emerson's genius straining against Emerson's model. They are accompanied, appropriately enough in this period of transition, by some of the best journalizing Emerson has ever done, which seems in contrast like the production of Emerson's genius yielding to Emerson's inclination: the work of the laziness of genius. "The Parnassian nag I rode I percieve has thrown me, and I have been bestriding a hobby" (JMN II: 329). A fair sample of his work in this lower but more congenial activity is this series of remarks loosely centered around Benjamin Franklin:

> Franklin was political economist, a natural philosopher, a moral philosopher, & a statesman. Invents & dismisses subtle theories (e.g. of the Earth) with extraordinary ease. Unconscious of any mental effort in detailing the profoundest solutions of phenomena & therefore makes no parade. He writes to a friend when aet. 80 "I feel as if I was intruding among posterity when I ought to be abed & asleep. I look upon death to be as necessary to the Constitution as Sleep. We shall rise refreshed in the morning."

> "Many," said he, "forgive injuries, but none ever forgave contempt."— See Edin. Rev.

> That age abounded in greatness: Carnot, Moreau, Bonaparte, &c, Johnson, Gibbon, &c, Washington, &c.

> Institutions are a sort of homes. A man may wander long with profit, if he come home at last but a perpetual Vagrant is not honoured. Men may alter & improve their laws so they fix them at last.

> "Humanity does not consist in a squeamish ear." Fox

> Men in this age do not produce new works but admire old ones; Are content to leave the fresh pastures awhile, & to chew the cud of thought in the shade.

> "A Great empire like a great cake is most easily diminished at the edges." Franklin. (JMN II: 208)

20. Perhaps we should note here that these passages also exhibit many more marks of revisions than do their earlier counterparts. This I think means not that Emerson was working harder at his prose but that he was thinking of his journal as the fit place for recording the earlier stages of composition, the lacunae and erasures and unresolved word choices that open up such extraordinary imaginative space behind them; that is, he was in this respect also coming to see what is revealed by examining the part as if it were the whole, the means as if it were the end.

The passage reveals Emerson's movement from a commonplace book of parts to a journal of wholes. The remark on the abounding greatness of "that age" is formally dependent on its context because of "that." The rest of the remarks are formally independent: nothing in their formulation links them to one another. Each stands by itself. The change is easy enough to formulate but has large consequences; it implies Emerson's movement from the Lockean circle to the Emersonian parabola, from a world of topics to a universe of microcosms.

Let us look at the passage more closely, so as to sense some of the pleasures this new practice offers. Emerson is drawing on an 1806 *Edinburgh Review* article by Francis Jeffrey. The article is diffuse and schematic; Emerson has picked out its most interesting assertion and its most memorable quotation. Moreover, the article presents the note on Franklin's unpretentious facility as a theorist in a section on Franklin the scientist, the quotation from the letter to Whatley in one on Franklin the man of letters and moral philosopher. The two Franklins are not brought into contact, and indeed the weakness of the article is precisely that in it Franklin's faculties are severed so easily from one another. By Emerson's juxtaposition of them the gracious precision of the jest on old age is thereby related to, indeed seems to *exemplify* those subtle theories invented and dismissed with extraordinary ease, and we are reminded that however we distinguish among the various faculties of a single subject, they must in the end be one as the subject is one. Even as a reader, that is, Emerson has brought us a good way out of the Lockean world of topics.

As a writer he takes us a good deal farther. Let us look in particular at the remarks on the age and on institutions. Implicitly they make Franklin the representative of a heroic past, which is explicitly contrasted with a contemplative present; yet this characterization of the present age cannot be read as an unqualified condemnation. Emerson is keeping a *journal,* and these remarks are his actions; it is *Emerson* who is both performing and critiquing the contemplation he sees as characteristic of his age. And keeping in mind this performative aspect of his writing we note more carefully that, after all, chewing the cud of thought in the shade is not so much a declination from as the necessary sequel to grazing on fresh pastures. Then too, the sayings quoted of Franklin and Fox refine our sense of "new works"—which, it seems, are done by the makers of delicate epigrams. This is by itself something to know, and Franklin's epigram in particular reveals, surprisingly, not bold vision but tactical adroitness, suggesting that new works are among other things the works of politicians; Fox's further suggests that such works may seem harsh and reminds us of what they may cost. Finally there is the remark on institutions. Juxtaposed to the remark on the greatness of Franklin's age, it suggests a notion of Franklin as a member of a class, a man in the end enmeshed in institutions as he was surrounded by greatness; and the notion is acutely true of Franklin, who in fact wandered long with profit but came home at last. This account of progression from a freer stage to one more bound leads us back to the remark on the procession of ages and perhaps to some more general perception of the laws of sequence: from individuality, fluidity, vagracy, innovation, consumption to institutions and men living in them, admiration, contemplation, rumination.

We should perhaps note in concluding this section that it is precisely in the context of a reader that the pleasures and insights we have described are imaginable. The Lockean commonplace book is a stockroom for a writer; it is no more a book than is a scholar's collection of index cards. The book Emerson has now found out how to make borrows a good deal from the Lockean model; but it is essentially a *book*, and the Lockean model is now not its authority but one among its sources.[21]

Strayings and Temptations

Wideworld 13, the last of the Wideworld series, is followed by a volume numbered 14 but unnamed. We may take this as a signal of the character of the succeeding volumes. On the one hand, they are not any longer assigned a topic, and they contain much writing like that of the Franklin passage. On the other hand, they contain also Emerson's backslidings in the direction of quarterly essays; the new

21. Interestingly, the development of this practice in the journal antedates by some years the articulation of its rationale in Emerson's consciousness. Compare Stephen Whicher: "Emerson came late into his force. The years recorded in the first two volumes of his journal—those before his resignation from the Second Church—show little distinction of style or thought. . . . In 1830, however, his thought begins to move, until, at the close of that year and the opening of the next, irresistible suggestions of sentiment come on him in a rush. . . . In the year 1831 Emerson came into his intellectual majority" (*Freedom and Fate* [Philadelphia: University of Pennsylvania Press, 1953], pp. 3, 19, and 23). Whicher's sense of the *shape* of Emerson's life is still pretty much our own, and its persistence is I think a further consequence of our disinclination to read Emerson's journal as the work of a writer looking for his form.

practice is not consistent. Nor does it seem to occupy the center of Emerson's consciousness, though the debate over indolence diligence shifts somewhat in favor of indolence.[22] Rather the new practice still seems the product of a powerful but sporadic and unarticulated impulse, an impulse no longer restrained by the Lockean model but not as yet capable of creating a model of its own.

The remaining portion of this chapter proposes certain elements of a story about how Emerson comes to understand and to systematize the practice he has developed. To tell that story in full would be to rehearse much that is familiar in Emerson's biography, for surely, say, his marriage with Ellen Tucker and his encounter with Coleridge contribute to the development of the resolute self-consciousness manifested in the opening statements of Journal A in 1834. Our goal here is narrower: to look closely at the intervening formal changes in the journal as we might look at the evolution of Pound's poetry from "Sestina: Altaforte" to "Mauberley," that is, to see those changes as situated along the path of an intelligence looking for a form.

The Temptations of the Sermon

The first of those changes takes place during Emerson's brief career in the ministry. The JMN editors describe the episode as follows:

> The journals and notebooks of these years are fewer and less packed than those in the preceding six years. A major reason is that although

---

22. Thus see JMN III: 136 and L I: 233.
An epitome of Emerson's progress along this line is articulated by the progress in the journal of a favorite passage of Horace: "Incipe. Vivendi recte qui prorogat horam,/ Rusticus expectat dum defluat amnis; at ille/ labitur ac labetur in omne volubilis aevum." ("Begin now! The man who puts off the time of living wisely [is] a peasant waiting for the river to run dry; but the river flows and will continue to flow, rolling on forever.") This is an exhortation to discipline; the peasant waits for the river to run dry rather than taking control of its course, just as we let life take its course with us rather than controlling it by the agency of wisdom. Emerson quotes it first as a concluding epigraph to Wideworld 3 (JMN I: 90). He quotes it next at the close of the dedication of Wideworld 9 (JMN II: 76): an exhortation to work for human progress. He quotes it again as a concluding epigraph to Wideworld 9 (JMN II: 101). He quotes it in Wideworld 10 as exemplifying the course of time (JMN II: 106). So far it has remained an exhortation; Emerson is on the side of the rightly living man, not on that of the river. But then, in Wideworld 13 (JMN II: 250), he suddenly changes sides: "the stream of liberty which the Holy Alliance are striving to *dam*—at ille/ labitur et labetur in omne volubilis aevum." Now he is on the side of the flux, just at the moment that in his journal he ceases trying to take control of the world through topics and surrenders to its flux of "particular impressions."

> Emerson wrote down many an idea for a sermon in his journals, as
> time went on he wrote the sermons independently. He found in the
> sermon the outlet for his thought formerly sought in *"theme, poem, or*
> *review."* In effect the sermons in manuscript are different versions of
> his journals—structured, more formal, prepared for a live audience,
> but still the embodiment of what he was thinking from day to day.
> (JMN III: ix)

But this account rests on the assumption that the journals are essentially *auxiliary* to Emerson's real literary production. We have all
along been proceeding on the assumption that the journals *are* Emerson's literary production. How then might we tell the story of his
silence?

In the period of his ministry Emerson created a new literary economy and a new literary vocation. He had been principally a diarist.
He now became a sermon writer, and the sermon supplanted the
diary.[23] This it could do because in its calendrical regularity it both
occupied the diarist's time and imitated the diary's form. That is: it
was not only a text to which the journal might contribute; it was a text
that the journal might become, and indeed did become. And what
does it mean that it underwent this transformation? Emerson the
diarist became Emerson the preacher. That is to say that the pressure
of his vocation led Emerson to become what he had so artfully
avoided becoming of his own election. His particular ministry, in one
of Boston's great churches, had very much the look of a Lockean
career; and in becoming predominantly a writer of sermons he became that public speaker for whom the Lockean commonplace book
was the fit instrument.

In the end, of course, Emerson left the ministry. He left it, the
biographies tell us, in consequence of his principled reluctance to
administer communion, on the ground that it was a merely historical
ordinance. But that decision also restored him to a space in which he
could develop his stubbornly dualistic literary economy. We remember that Emerson the minister was a fine orator but an indifferent
counselor. We may if we like allegorize this and say that the ministry
entailed for him a predominant focus on one of his two audiences he
later kept in balance; for, as we shall see, the distinguishing feature in

---

23. Especially vivid indications of that supplantation are two remarks referring the
reader of the journal to the sermons: "for the rest see Sermon LXVI" (JMN III: 180)
and "see this matter at large in Sermon 93" (JMN III: 205). Clearly the journal is no
independent text if what is begun in it is finished elsewhere.

Emerson's later economy is precisely its balancing of congregation against inner circle, of essay and lecture against journal. The ministry was the occasion for him to experiment with one of the more usual systems of literary production: a processing of private raw materials for the sake of a public finished product. He left it to develop his own system and his journal.

The Temptations of the Travel Book

In Chapter XVII of *Wilhelm Meister*, the itinerant Wilhelm promises his father "a copious journal of his travels, with all the required geographical, statistical, and mercantile remarks."[24] The promise is dictated by filial piety, but the accomplishing of it goes against Wilhelm's nature: "as soon as he commenced the actual work of composition, he became aware that he had much to say about emotions and thoughts . . . but not a word concerning outward objects" (294). Wilhelm's friend Laertes then proposes to him to fabricate a journal to the father's taste from the books of travels that are Laertes' favorite reading. Things go well; indeed they go surprisingly well, because the feigned journal comes near to making Wilhelm into a real journalist:

> In the marvellous composition of those travels, which he had at first engaged with as it were in jest, and was now carrying on in conjunction with Laertes, his mind had by degrees grown more attentive to the circumstances and the every-day life of the actual world than it was wont. He now, for the first time, felt how pleasant and how useful it might be to become participator in so many trades and requisitions, and to take a hand in diffusing activity and life into the deepest nooks of the mountains and forests of Europe. (304)

But then Wilhelm's father dies, and his brother Werner, much impressed with the feigned journal, proposes to Wilhelm to come home and join him in business. This is too much for Wilhelm, who confesses the ruse and writes of the journal,

> though in words I know the objects it relates to, and more of the like sort, I by no means understand them, or can occupy myself about them. What good were it for me to manufacture perfect iron, while my own breast is full of dross? (318–19)

24. Johann Wolfgang von Goethe, *Wilhelm Meister's Apprenticeship and Travels*, tr. Thomas Carlyle [vol. 22 in Carlyle's *Works* (Boston: Dana Estes, n.d., Centennial Memorial Edition)], p. 294; further citations identified by page number in the text.

plained, that 'ride as far or as fast as he would, the milestones were all alike, & told the same number.' (JMN II: 179)

The European trip is then a considerable temptation, because it presents a glittering opportunity for Emerson to do something he does well but does not esteem, and to do it in the space in which he has learned to do something altogether different. Wilhelm's character comes near to undergoing a fundamental alteration through his *simulation* of travel writing; ought we not to look for some large problem in Emerson's *practice* of it?

On his arrival in Malta, Emerson writes,

> I bring myself to sea, to Malta, to Italy, to find new affinities between me & my fellowmen, to observe narrowly the affections, weaknesses, surprises, hopes, doubts, which new sides of the panorama shall call forth *in me*. Mean sneakingly mean would be this philosophy, a reptile unworthy of the name, if *self* be used in the low sense, but as self means Devil so it means God. I speak of the Universal Man to whose colossal dimensions each particular bubble can by its birthright expand. (JMN IV: 68; first italics mine, second Emerson's)

Emerson the mature writer produced *English Traits* in accordance with this exhortation. But Emerson the young man on his first trip to Europe produced a book of reportage: calendrically regular in its entries, and full of anecdotes and vivid observations.

> Then we went to Dionysius' Ear; a huge excavation into the hard rock [in Syracuse] which I am not going to describe. Poor People were making twine in it & my ear was caught on approaching it by the loud noise made by their petty wheels in the vault. A little beyond the entrance the floor was covered with a pool of water. We found a twine maker who very readily took us, one after another on his shoulders into the recess 250 ft, & planted us on dry land at the bottom of the cave. We shouted & shouted & the cave bellowed & bellowed; the twine maker tore a bit of paper in the middle of the cave, & very loud it sounded; then they fired a pistol at the entrance & we had our fill of thunder. . . . (JMN IV: 122–123)
>
> The Italians use the Superlative too much. Mr Landor calls them the nation of the *issimi*. A man to tell me that this was the same thing I had before, said "E l'istessissima cosa;" and at the trattoria, when I asked if the cream was good, the waiter answered, "Stupendo." They use three negatives; it is good Italian to say, 'Non dite nulla a nessuno. . . .' (JMN IV: 176)

Early in the trip this sort of effect took considerable work; the earlier travel journals were written first in pencil, then "revised with great care and in [Emerson's] most legible hand later in ink" (JMN IV: 102). As of June 1833, however, Emerson writes only one draft. The JMN editors explain the change on the supposition that by this time Emerson "had caught up his journal" (JMN IV: 185). This is possible; but is it not also possible to think simply that by now Emerson had learned his job? The travel journals present not a philosopher rebelling against an unphilosophical model but a gifted apprentice learning his craft.

Or rather, they present Emerson doing both. The journal recording Emerson's travels records also numerous exhortations to travel more philosophically. "How," Emerson asks while still at sea, "comes my speculative pencil down to so near a level with the horizon of life, which commonly proses above?" (JMN IV: 110). He goes to the opera in Catania, but finds the entrance fee of three taris "too much for the whistle" and defends his preference for his inward theater, his "own comedy & tragedy" (JMN IV: 132). In Naples he defends himself against Naples: "and what if it is Naples, it is only the same world of cake & ale. . . . Here's for the plain old Adam, the simple genuine Self against the whole world" (JMN IV: 141).

These exhortations are quickly enough flouted, however. They are after all only exhortations and affect the texture of the record hardly at all, which remains essentially an itinerary. But Emerson the journalist and philosopher is carrying on his resistance in other ways also, though these are evident only if we attend to certain dry bibliographical data. Throughout the trip Emerson kept more than one journal concurrently. This was to be his occasional practice all his life long; but seldom did he produce such a bewildering disarray. He kept Notebook Q before, during, and after the European trip. The Notebooks Sicily, Italy, Italy and France, Scotland and England, and Sea 1833 each record a part of the trip; all, then, overlap Q. Notebook Scotland and England does some overlapping on its own; Emerson used it in 1832 for miscellaneous notes and on the voyage out for accounts. Notebook France and England contains Italian language exercises, rought drafts for entries in Notebook Italy and France, and also some passages on Emerson's English adventures not revised for Notebook Scotland and England, in particular much of Emerson's encounter with Coleridge; Pocket Diary II contains mostly *memoranda* but also an anecdote of Burns the younger.

Notebook Q is a sort of philosophical monitor on the other books; seldom in it does Emerson's pencil "come down so near to the horizon of life" as it does in the others, and in nearly overlapping passages it is characteristically the version in Q that presents Emerson looking inward rather than outward.[27] But we can see a more general resistance to the genre he is doing so well at simply in the multiplicity of books itself. That genre is, as we have noted, *essentially* a single chronological sequence, *essentially* a single narrative; but here is Emerson creating not one narrative but five. Yes, he seems to be saying, he will write *Emerson on the Grand Tour;* but he will make the Grand Tour into a series of fits and starts, and his narrative a pointillistic series of images.

In later life Emerson travels widely and often, and is less troubled by these problems. The poem on the travel-spirit "Una" suggests his mature solution to them:

> At home a deeper thought may light
> The inward sky with chrysolite,
> And I greet from far the ray,
> Aurora of a dearer day.
>
> But if upon the seas I sail,
> Or trundle on the glowing rail,
> I am but a thought of hers,
> Loveliest of travellers.[28]

But this easy separation of faculties is impossible for the younger Emerson, presumably because he is at this time uncertain of the form

27. Thus in Notebook Sicily Emerson writes on February 16, 1833, "to be sure there is plenty of superstition. Every where indulgence is offered, and on one convent on our way home I read this inscription over the gate, 'Indulgentia plenaria, quotidiana, perpetua, pro vivis et defunctis.' This is almost too frank, may it please your holiness" (JMN IV: 117). In Q, under the heading "1833, February" (even the more general date is indicative), he writes, "I am now pleased abundantly with St John's Church in Valetta. Welcome these new joys. Let my American eye be a child's again to these glorious picture books. The chaunting friars, the carved ceilings, the Madonnas & Saints, they are lively oracles, quotidiana et perpetua" (JMN IV: 84).

For a similar division of travel journals by function see Memo St. Augustine and Journal 1826–1828 in JMN III; for a comment of Emerson's on the underlying rationale, see JMN V: 82: "the life of a contemplator is that of a reporter. He has three or four books before him & now writes in this now in that other what is incontinuously said by one or the other of his classes of thought."

28. In Edward Waldo Emerson, ed., *The Complete Works of Ralph Waldo Emerson* (Boston: Houghton Mifflin, 1903–1904; Centenary Edition), 12 vols., IX: 211; see also Paul O. Williams, "Meaning in Emerson's 'Una,' " *Emerson Society Quarterly* 31, p. 48. Henceforth the *Works* will be abbreviated as W and the *Quarterly* as ESQ.

to be given his "inward sky." On his first Grand Tour, the conventions of the travel book do not supplement but encroach upon the journal he is learning how to keep.

In the *Letters to a Young Poet,* Rilke writes to Franz Kappus that to know whether or not he is really a poet, he should for a year try his best to keep from writing poetry; and that in a way is precisely what Emerson has done. He is feeling his way towards becoming the greatest American diarist of the century. In the course of his ministry, he experiments with being something other than a diarist; he undertakes a career as a writer in a genre to which the diary is subordinated. In the course of his European travels, he experiments with being a different sort of diarist; he is a writer in a genre by which the diary is threatened. The episode of the ministry has raised the question, what public career will further my growth as a diarist? The Grand Tour has brought into Emerson's consciousness the question, What sort of journal am I keeping? Shortly after his return, in December of 1833, he emerges for the first time as Emerson the diarist we know and as Emerson the lecturer. These actions have the inevitability of solutions to geometrical problems. In the career of lecturer, with the notable openness of the form of the American lyceum lecture, he finds a career in the context of which Emerson the diarist can flourish. In the mature journal he finds the form in which the energies of Emerson the diarist are animated. He has henceforth that clarity of purpose experienced only by those who have found out their vocation by denying it.

A Conscious Beginning

We date Emerson's mature journals from 1833 for two reasons. The first is that as of that moment the journal exhibits consistently rather than sporadically the diaristic qualities we have identified as idiomatically Emersonian; there are no more backslidings till the journal itself comes to an end. The second is that Journal A, the first of the mature journals, has the look of a conscious beginning.

What traits make for that look and what do they tell us?[29] The first

29. An obvious one would seem the letter A by which the first of the new journals is titled, but Linda Allardt suggests on the evidence of the lecture notebooks that Emerson did not give the volume that title until some time after the close of the "Philosophy of History" in March 1837 (JMN XII: xxxvi).

are the changes in physical format: henceforth Emerson's blank books are bought rather than made and are of relatively uniform size (JMN IV:249). Journal making remains an artisanal task; but now the artisan is at least going to buy professional tools.

More suggestive are new volume's epigraphs and first entry. These are the epigraphs:

> Ch'apporta mane, e lascia sera
>
> Not of men neither by man
>
> May I "consult the auguries of time
> And through the human heart explore my way
> And look & listen"[30]

Together the epigraphs suggest the commitment to chronological narrative, to individuality, and to sacred vocation that we have associated with the influence of Mary Moody Emerson. But then we turn to the opening declaration:

> This Book is my Savings Bank. I grow richer because I have somewhere to deposit my earnings; and fractions are worth more to me because corresponding fractions are waiting here that shall be made integers by their addition. (JMN IV: 250–51)

Here we have the commitment to usefulness, to productivity, and to collection that we have associated with the influence of John Locke. Neither influence has been suppressed; rather both have been intelligently thematized.

But the most striking evidence of Emerson's new consciousness, though also the most abstruse, is his development of an idiomatic system of indexing. Let us take a moment to set this development in its context. We recall that Locke's account of commonplacing instructs the reader to begin with the index, at once the auxiliary and the *telos* of the book. What is Emerson's actual practice? Wideworld 1 is set up by the Lockean scheme (though perhaps, as the editors note, only in 1821). In most of the remaining Wideworld volumes, topics are noted in bottom or side margins but not gathered into a general volume index. Wideworld 9 (1822–23) and XVIIIA are Locke-indexed, but very incompletely. From the end of the Wideworld series till Journal A

---

30. (1) "What brings the morning and leaves behind the evening": Dante's phrase for the sun in *Paradiso* XXVII: 138; (2) Gal. I: 1; (3) Wordsworth, "Not 'mid the World's vain objects."

we get a mix of foot indexing and very fragmentary Lockean indexing.[31] Presumably Emerson declines to use the Lockean system because of its museum air and its association with limited topicality, its ordered world of definable, severable topics, its implied distinctions between the diligent and the idle, the serious and trivial. Emerson's own indices have no such associations, but they are very bad tools; to consult the index the reader has to read the book.

The system worked out for Journal A is both a good tool and an idiomatically Emersonian tool. First, it is composed, unlike Locke's, on a blank and unlined page; it suggests, that is, not a set of categories embedded within a grid but a structure built *ex nihilo*.[32] Its category names are taken not only from nouns but also from verbs and adjectives; they allow for invention and variation. It is done after the book is complete, rather than in conjunction with the individual entry; it thus suggests leisure rather than demanding efficiency, and presents the finding of a category as a complex rather than a simple activity. It permits multiple naming for topically ambivalent passages, or rather it acknowledges the perception that all passages are topically ambivalent. It justifies Emerson's striking assertion that "classification is a delight."

Let us look in particular at the index to Journal N.[33] Locke's brief, dismissive account of the process of finding a category suggests that he thought of it as something like finding the right spot on the shelf for a book in a well-ordered library. For Emerson classifying was inventing, and nowhere more clearly than in the numerous instances in which a single utterance is indexed under more than one heading and thus conceived of as more than one entity. One passage is indexed under "Community" and "Individualism" another under "Affirmative," "Few Steps," and "Greatness." (Again, we should note even the *grammatical* variety among the names; indexing may be pigeonholing, but Emerson seems determined to create pigeonholes of di-

31. The quotation books for the period show a somewhat different picture; the JMN editors describe it as "an attempt on his part to organize the entries more carefully, so that the random lustre-collecting of the early books gives way to the topic headings and careful indexing of the later ones" (JMN VI: ix). Even here, however, the impression of resistance to Lockean efficiency is strong—some of the principles of organization make use of the books almost impossible—and not until 1829, for Encyclopedia, does Emerson make use of a system permitting easy access to the quotations he has gathered.

32. Compare L I: 59: "Poetry is my delight/ Exceedingly bright/ My desire to write/ It in the night/ on paper white."

33. I choose this example because it is published in facsimile in JMN VIII (facing p. 328).

verse sizes and shapes: three bare abstract nouns, one concrete noun attended by an equally concrete adjective, and one adjective all alone.) The following passage is indexed under "Education," "Faith," and "Fate," and as we consider the passage in the light of the various rubrics it turns about like a many-faceted jewel.

> But he is shallow who rails at men and their contrivances & does not see Divinity behind all their institutions and all their fetches, even behind such as are odious & paltry, they are documents of beauty also. The practice of Prayer is not philosophical,—there is somewhat of absurd & ridiculous in it to the eye of Science; it is juvenile, and, like plays of children, though nonsense, yet very useful and educative nonsense. Well so with all our things,—the most solemn & large,—as Commerce, Government, Church, Marriage; and so with the history of every man's dinner today, & the ways by which he is to come at it. (JMN VIII: 281)

As we regard it as bearing on education, we note particularly Emerson's sense of the practical use of apparent absurdity, the instruction offered by all phenomena; as we regard it as bearing on fate, we note not the instruction but the *power* underlying human contrivance; as we regard it as bearing on faith, we note the perspective of the writer, the *trust* in that power and in that education. To assign any passage to any topic is of course an act of interpretation and not the passive performance of a mechanical task that Locke's account would suggest; to assign one passage to three topics is to *exploit* the interpretive possibilities of the act, almost to play with them, to proclaim a consciousness of intepretative power.

But as assigning a particular utterance to a particular topic or topics is a reading of the utterance, a weighting of it in a particular direction, so the volume index as a whole is a reading of the book. For what after all does an index tell us? First, and most practically, it tells us where to locate passages on a subject of interest to us, should we know what that subject is and know how to name it. But also it makes an argument about the organization of the book; it says that this passage is to be associated with these other passages, that they form a group, that there is some reason for considering them together; it creates themes. We note, reading the *Scarlet Letter,* the three scenes on the scaffold, one at the beginning, one at the middle, one at the end; we judge them to have something in common with one another, and we extract from the book this subordinate sequence of it. So Emerson's index. The passage we looked at is indexed under education; this suggests that we read it in conjunction with this other passage:

Men are great in their own despite. They achieve a certain greatness, but it was while they were toiling to achieve another conventional one. The boy at college apologizes for not learning the tutor's task, & tries to learn it, but stronger nature gives him Otway & Massinger to read, or betrays him into a stroll to Mount Auburn in study-hours. The poor boy instead of thanking the gods and slighting the Mathematical tutor, ducks before the functionary, & poisons his own fine pleasures by a perpetual penitence. Well at least let that one never brag of the choice he made; as he might have well done, if he had known what he did when he was doing it. (JMN VIII: 266)

If we join the two passages together, each illuminates the other, and both compose a meditation on education as accident, as fringe bene-fit, as illumination universally available and universally slighted or scorned. But suppose we follow the suggestions of the index entry "Fate" and consider these passages:

Fate, yes, our music box only plays certain tunes & never a sweeter strain but we are assured that our barrel is not a dead but a live barrel,— nay, is only a part of the tune & changes like that . . .

Conservatism stands on this, that a man cannot jump out of his skin; & well for him that he cannot, for his skin is the world; & the stars of heaven do hold him there; in the folly of men glitters the wisdom of God. (JMN VIII: 251–52; the two passages occur in succession but on different pages of the manuscript volume.)

Now we have made a different sampling, traced a different pattern— considered, to continue the earlier analogy, not the three scenes on the scaffold but the series of conversations between Hester and Dimmesdale, one of which is coincident with one of the scenes upon the scaffold. The passage on education, with its telling comments on our unwillingness to learn the truths daily if haphazardly presented to us, becomes part of a meditation on fate, thus identified as one of the journal's themes, its *continua*, in which we see these vainly neglected truths in their *power*, see our unwillingness to learn from them as one of a number of examples of our inability not to benefit from necessity but to resist benefiting from it. And so with each of the index head-ings, each identifying a theme, a thread in the tapestry of a book—or, rather, not identifying but creating it, the index as a whole creating the flexible thematic repertory of the particular volume, the idiomati-cally Emersonian index making possible the idiomatically Emer-sonian journal.

The Emersonian journal is arguably the genre the Transcendentalists did best at; not only Emerson's journal but many others of its sort as well are their authors' best work, among them Thoreau's, Alcott's, Fuller's, and Charles King Newcomb's. Of the great English and German Romantics, on the other hand, surprisingly few kept journals of literary distinction, and of those who did, none kept journals of Emerson's sort. Why should this have been so?

In 1816, the German Romantic poet August von Platen, then already keeping a diary, resolved to keep simultaneously with it a commonplace book: a place for "ideas, plans, reflections, remarks on various subjects such as I think worth the transcribing":

> My diary will not be broken off in consequence of this waste-book; seldom have I recorded here individual thoughts of that sort, as they commonly arise on walks and then easily vanish again, since these pages have always retained a certain connectedness and precisely on this account could not be very rich in reflections—all too often it happened that one object of thought excluded all others and filled the pages itself, which accordingly had to lose much by way of diversity.[34]

This is a commonsensical argument, resting on commonsensical distinctions between private and public and between work and life. It is moreover one borne out in both English and Continental practice. The two great English Romantic journals are presumably Byron's and Dorothy Wordsworth's; neither is a workplace. The great English Romantic workplace is presumably Coleridge's notebooks; they are no journal.

How distinctive then Emerson's enterprise can look! To keep a waste book, a miscellany, is to acknowledge the transience of thoughts, the necessity to record them lest they be forgotten, perhaps the possible fruitfulness of their accidental juxtaposition, and that the Transcendentalists did; but what of the practice of organizing this miscellany chronologically and intertwining it with the record of a life? Emerson has chosen to put in his book not only the thousand scraps of reading and writing a commonplace book must contain but also those contingent data it must exclude. Or: Emerson has chosen to put in his diary not only the continuous record of his life and thought but also the thousand evanescent thoughts by which that record is complicated. In his book, that is, the private and public, the eternal and the contingent, the life and the work will inevitably collide and fuse. Lofty speculations

34. Hocke, *Das Europaeische Tagebuch*, pp. 717–18.

must be shown to have arisen in time, in a sequence of other events, from the mind of a particular human being.

The Transcendentalist practice suggests two characteristic and complementary American attitudes: an inclination to subordinate all activities to the recording of a life, and a reluctance to separate the work of art from the life of the artist, for fear, as Thoreau put it, "that the work of art should be at the expense of the man." In America all art tends towards the condition of autobiography, and all autobiography to the condition of life, but equally all life tends towards the condition of autobiography and all autobiography towards the condition of art. Emerson in inventing the Transcendentalist journal found not only an apt synthesis of conflicting influences but an apt form for the Transcendentalist vision. [35]

35. For an alternative explanation of the paucity of European Romantic diaries see Boerner, *Tagebuch*, p. 45: "Despite their predisposition for the fragmentary, the Romantics resorted only seldom to the intrinsic jumble of the diary. One reason may be that a fragment in the Romantic sense is something broken off intentionally and thus something not susceptible of completion, whereas the diary presents a structure always perceived in its ongoing growth." On the Romantic fragment see also "The Journal and the Aphorism Book," pp. 107ff.

III

The Form of
the Mature Journal

Introduction

The Russian formalist Tynianov remarks that underlying literary history is the concept of the evolution of *systems*. Tzvetan Todorov, quoting that remark, continues:

> Changes in literary discourses are not isolated; each affects the whole system, and thus eventually brings about the substitution of one system for another. We may define a literary *period* as the time during which a certain system continues relatively unchanged.[1]

We may learn from this that to describe such a text as Emerson's journal is implicitly to locate it within the systems to which it belongs. I take these to be the Emersonian literary system; the genre of the Transcendentalist journal; and, most suggestively, the literary texts pertinent to Emerson's literary period, in particular of course those most similar to, and thus most sharply illustrating, the Emersonian journal, that is, the aphorism book and the quotation book. The following leisurely, overlapping essays set the journal within each of these systems in turn.

One goal of these essays is to make a case for the journal as a work of art. Now this is something rather different than to make a case for a despised writer or text. When Eliot revives Donne or Marvell, his proper strategy is the polemically celebratory description and analysis of particular, putatively exemplary passages, for an audience pre-

1. Todorov, *Dictionnaire*, pp. 190–91.

61

sumed to have ignored or undervalued the virtues he seeks to establish. In the present instance, however, no such attitude can be presumed; readers of Emerson's journals have characteristically taken and proclaimed intense pleasure in them. The problem here is to alter not taste or judgment but mentality. Readers' pleasure in the journals has so far been sterile, for lack of categories in which to develop it. The case made here for the journals is an attempt to supply them; it presents notions in the context of which the journal we already know and cherish can become not only a source of pleasure but also an object of critical thought.

A fringe benefit of the enterprise is a rehabilitation of Emerson the critic. Traditionally we have begun our judgment of him in that capacity from the presumption that Emerson's literary *performance* is his lectures and essays.[2] Inevitably we have perceived the real flaws of that performance, and inevitably perceived also that the performance is in some way at odds with the theory. There has followed the usual result of contemplating apparent hypocrisy. When Matthiessen finds that Emerson's practice and his theory are at odds, Emerson becomes for him simply a man not living by the standards he preached: a failed writer and a windy critic.

My own reading of Emerson the critic begins from my judgment that Emerson's chief literary performance is his journal. Now Emerson is a better journalizer than he is an essayist. This fact alone gives one a certain initial tolerance for Emerson's notorious critical abstractions. But then a strange thing happens. Many of those abstractions turn out, when applied to the journal, to be remarkably concrete; they seemed vague because we had no literary object adequate to exemplify or illustrate them. Thus the numerous exaltations of nature over art seem more telling when we imagine them defending (and defining) a form partly constituted not by art but by chance. Viewed in the light of his entire literary practice, and in particular with reference to the heterodox masterpiece at its center, Emerson becomes a much shrewder and more concrete aesthetician. Once seen as an extremist, he becomes a precisian.

One thing this series of essays will *not* do is pay much attention to the manner in which Emerson altered passages of the journal for use in the lectures and essays. Such alteration is notoriously among Em-

2. See for example René Wellek, *A History of Modern Criticism* (New Haven: Yale University Press, 1965), III: 163–76; Vivian Hopkins, *Spires of Form* (Cambridge: Harvard University Press, 1951); F. O. Matthiessen, *American Renaissance*, pp. 3–75.

erson's chief means of composition, and the question of what happens to particular passages under adaptation has already attracted some interest and will no doubt with the completed publication of the journals attract much more.[3] It has not, however, yielded much light; and it is, I think, not likely to. The reason is that while examining the process we have also been misconceiving it. We have considered Emerson as the reviser of a draft for publication. But the journals are no draft; they are a text. A primary fact about Emerson the writer is that he created *two* texts, two large formal structures, for the same words. If we are to compare individual passages used in both structures, we ought to do so with a sense of what both structures are. If a maxim of Goethe's turns up both in *Wilhelm Meister* and in the *Maximen und Reflexionen*, our proper comparative interest is not between the two *versions* of the maxim but between the two *genres* into which it has been incorporated.

Accordingly, though a consideration of relations between particular journal *passages* and their adaptations in the lectures and essays is peripheral here, the consideration of relations between the journal *qua* text and the essays *qua* text is central. Tynianov's remark holds good for the study of an individual; there too we have to consider the whole: the Emersonian literary system. That we have not done so is responsible for certain grand misconstructions of the essays. We have seen them in isolation from, or, at best, in superordination to, the very texts they need to be compared with, on a basis of equality. We have, for example, considered them fragmentary or associative or solipsistic, and we have said as much of Emerson's mind, not having located either the essays or the author within the totality of his production. One goal of the following essays is to rectify these errors by setting each of Emerson's forms within that totality.

Another is to understand these forms, and in particular the form of the journal, as responses to Emerson's historical world; among the Emersons these essays have in mind is an intelligent artist living through America's transition from agrarian to industrial capitalism, and the forms that that intelligent artist devised are understood as apt responses to that transition, and in particular as a critique of the America coming into being from the viewpoint of the America just passing out of view. In that sense these essays are very much in

3. See, for example, Buell, *Literary Transcendentalism*, pp. 285–88, and Glen Johnson, "Emerson's Craft of Revision," *Studies in the American Renaissance* 1980, pp. 51–72.

accord with our current rethinking of Emerson and with our rethinking of the American Renaissance generally. As Sacvan Bercovitch writes,

> On some basic level, we will have to reconceive our so-called radical or subversive literary tradition as an insistent engagement with society, rather than a recurrent flight from it. In other words, we will have to re-historicize the ideal Americas projected in our major texts . . . we will have to re-see these fictions historically, in dynamic relation to the culture: neither as mirrors of their time, nor as lamps of the creative imagination, but as works of *ideological* mimesis, at once implicated in the society they resist, capable of overcoming the forces that compel their complicity, and nourished by the culture they often seem to subvert.[4]

Among the "ideal Americas projected in our major texts" is the world of Emerson's journal. It is, I think, not the most extreme of those worlds; but in its very moderation it escapes certain dangers. "What our major writers could not conceive," Bercovitch continues,

> either in their optative or in their tragic-ironic moods, was that the United States was neither utopia at best nor dystopia at worst . . . but a certain political system; that *in principle* no less than in practice the American Way was neither providential nor natural but one of many possible forms of society.[5]

Accordingly, their own literary worlds were as utopian or dystopian as the America they presumed themselves to be responding to: the universal corruption of Melville's *The Confidence Man;* Whitman's "wonderful cities and free nations we shall fetch as we go," Emerson's own "nation of men" in the vision at the end of "The American Scholar." The journal as form evokes no such images; it implies a temperate Jeremiad, a moderate utopia, and is, precisely on that account, among the most refractory critiques of nineteenth-century America.

Interlude: A Practical Note

The writer on Emerson's essays can say to the reader, "read this or that text and you will feel the force of what I mean." What can a writer

---

4. Bercovitch, "The Problem of Ideology in American Literary History," *Critical Inquiry* 12: 4 (Summer 1986), 642.

5. Ibid., p. 646.

on the sixteen volumes of Emerson's journals recommend to readers seeking to acquire some independent sense of the text those volumes constitute?

By far the best of the selections from the journals is Joel Porte's *Emerson in his Journals*. As a collection of interesting passages it can hardly be bettered. But it is, as such a collection must be, indifferent to the *form* of the material it draws on; and certain aspects of the following arguments deal with aspects of that form that Porte's selection of passages obscures. What feasible program of reading will reveal them? Emerson's own principle of presentation suggests the best answer. When he showed the journals to his friends and colleagues he showed them not a *selection* but a *section:* the journals from page ten to page twenty, or the journals of the year 1841. That is, he set boundaries but within those boundaries deleted nothing. Accordingly, my own recommendation to the reader would be to read any one of Emerson's *original* volumes from beginning to end. A particularly good example is Journal N (JMN VIII: 248–308 and Plate VII between pp. 328 and 329) because the editors have reproduced its index. Or perhaps a more Emersonian alternative would be simply to open any of the JMN volumes from IV to XIV, read for an afternoon a stretch of continuous pages, and then stop.

The Journal vs. the Essays

Is the Journal a Work of Art? (Part 1)

We know—and it is both the most important and the most misleading thing to know about the Emersonian literary system—that Emerson transcribed and adapted a good many passages of the journal for use in the lectures and essays; we might even describe these latter as being predominantly an arrangement of such transcriptions and adaptations, supplemented by new material written *ad hoc*. These facts have led us to make certain distinctions, to conceive certain beliefs regarding the Emersonian corpus. Thinking that the essays are wholes, we have conceived of the journals as fragments; thinking of the essays as finished products, as ends, we have regarded the journals as raw material, as means. Accordingly, we have been reluctant to regard as a literary work what we have understood as essentially *ancillary* to literary work. We have regarded the lectures and essays as literature; the journals, therefore, we have felt obliged to regard as something else.

Let us begin the long work of regarding the journals as literature by unsettling the distinction between raw material and finished product. Elaborated, the distinctions yields a dynamic model of the Emersonian literary system, a model we have so thoroughly assimilated that we describe it offhandedly, allude to it as to a truism it will not do to stress. Thus this precise yet almost apologetic formulation of Lawrence Buell's:

> The characteristic Transcendentalist pattern of composition, established by Emerson and imitated with varying degrees of success by Alcott, Thoreau, and Channing, was of course a threefold process of revision from journal to lecture to essay.[6]

As we imagine the process, its steps come in a necessary order: Emerson first writes a passage into the journal, then copies or modifies it for use in a lecture, then copies or modifies the lecture passage for use in an essay. Each stage subsumes the last, and at the end of the process, in the essay, the fluid has been solidified, the transient made permanent.

Against this model we can make three arguments. The first and most tentative concerns the essays, that is, the stage of print. Sometimes passages printed in one work are printed later in another. This is the exception, not the rule; but even *qua* exception the fact dissuades us from taking the essays as a *monumentum aere perennius*. They are not only cannibalized for; they are also cannibalized from.[7] And if the former happens more often than the latter, we ought perhaps to regard that pattern as expressing not Emerson's aesthetic satisfaction but his worldly prudence. What is printed is seldom made further use of not, perhaps, because it is in any artistic sense *final* but simply because it has been *read*, been made available—not because Emerson the artist has arrived at a goal but because the reader has been made part owner of the text.

Also, though again not often, the process sometimes goes in the opposite direction. Passages from the lectures turn up in later journals, passages from essays not only in later essays but also in later

6. Buell, *Literary Transcendentalism*, p. 280.
7. Thus, as the JMN editors indicate (JMN VIII: 254), a passage used in "Culture" (W VI: 142) turns up later in "Quotation and Originality" (W VII: 178) and still later in "Address at the Opening of the Concord Free Public Library" (W XI: 504).

journals and lectures.[8] The individual essay is already no indissoluble fabric; now the essays as a whole, the stage of print, is no longer everywhere the final stage of composition.

The second argument concerns the nature of the *transaction*, of the activity we casually refer to as "Emerson's use of journal material for lectures and essays." Let us imagine the history of a passage: written, used, thus used up, and discarded. But no; Emerson goes back to the journals again and again, as well as to the lectures and essays drawn from them. He goes back even to the early journals, the awkward *juvenalia* that most of us would gladly forget.[9] And most tellingly, he goes back to the *same passages* he has already used. Often, in fact, he goes back to passages extensively modified for early lectures and transcribes them in their original form for use in later lectures and in essays.[10] These passages if any ought to have been used up, because they were clearly *used;* but they were not. Nor should we regard this practice as manifesting happy second thoughts on the part of an older and wiser writer; "the first and third thoughts agree," runs one of Emerson's favorite proverbs, and though it is tempting to think of the later published version of such passages as their final form, nothing authorizes such a conclusion; all we can say is that it is the last one Emerson had occasion to give them, the journal passages themselves properly being conceived as still vital in their *cruda senectus*.[11]

A good emblem of the process of adaptation is the Emersonian use mark: a single vertical line drawn through a passage. It both obscures and highlights the passage it runs through, both interrupts it and calls

8. See, for example, JMN VII: 63, 209, and 337–38.
The last example is revelatory: a passage used in the lecture "Private Life," given January 8, 1840, turns up in the journal in an entry dated February 3, 1840. The editors write that it "may have been written prior to January 8, or it may have been copied from the lecture." Only an instinctive and unwarrantable belief that the public cannot be laid under tribute for the private makes the former speculation conceivable.
9. See JMN XII: xxii–xxiii. One striking example: a passage on John Adams used for the lecture "Old Age," published in the *Atlantic Monthly* in 1862, is drawn from a journal passage written in 1825 (JMN II: 333).
10. See JMN XII: xxi.
11. The one exception is Emerson's practice of *physical* cannibalization, his occasional tearing out of pages of the journal for use elsewhere. When the passage is gone physically its vitality is spent. But the practice of physical cannibalization is not restricted to Emerson's dealing with the journals; it is as common, indeed more common, in Emerson's dealing with his lecture manuscripts (see the notes to Stephen Whicher and Robert Spiller, eds., *The Early Lectures of Ralph Waldo Emerson* [Cambridge, Massachusetts: Harvard University Press, 1959–72; henceforth abbreviated EL], 3 vols.; and also Cabot, *Memoir*, II: 669).

attention to it. It indicates, that is, that a passage is *to be used,* not that it *has been used up:* an apt hieroglyph for the particular character of Emersonian use that is not exhaustion. It is then to be distinguished from the notation "printed," which Emerson interpolates sometimes after passages published in books. "Printed" says, prudently, "don't use this again; it's been printed." The use mark says only, "use this, *on this occasion,* for such and such a lecture or essay."

The last of the three arguments concerns the nature of the journals themselves, which cannot be properly described as raw material because so much of them is cooked. They are, that is, notoriously a book of quotations, that is, a book *for* which other books are cannibalized; they are as often a point of arrival as a point of origin. Even considered as a book exclusively of Emersonian utterances they are no universal and uniform first draft; they are a patchwork of copied and uncopied, revised and unrevised, corrected and uncorrected. Emerson transcribes and modifies passages from the journals not only for the lectures and essays but also for other journals, and not only from regular journals into topical ones but from one regular journal into the next, subjecting them to alterations similar to those practiced for the sake of the podium and the book. [12] So we cannot comfortably take the journals as one term of an antithesis, because it already contains the other.

Of the Emersonian literary system as a whole, [13] then, we can say that no passage can ever be considered as having attained its final form or arrived at its final context; that no passage is ever restricted to its initial context; that any passage can be reused; that no passage, by being reused, is ever exhausted. The distinction between raw material—or rough draft—and finished product is worse than useless in understanding Emerson's system of production, in which texts we normally regard

12. The practice is ubiquitous, but one particularly good example is JMN IV: 378: "A friend once told me that he never spent anything on himself without deserving the praise of disinterested benevolence." Emerson is here rephrasing an anecdote he tells earlier (JMN IV: 292) of his brother Charles, and in rephrasing it removing the name and thus the element of the personal just as he does in adapting journal passages for use in lectures and essays.

13. Minus, that is, the letters and the poems. Emerson did not habitually make copies of his letters, so *physically* they are not part of the system under discussion. The case of the poems is more complex. Drafts of them do occur in the journals; but most often a single poem in the journals corresponds to a single poem in the book or review. Emerson is, that is, using the journals for writing poems *in their entirety,* not for writing groups of lines later to be not only rewritten but also recombined. Appropriately enough, fairly often drafts of poems are written in pencil and later erased and overwritten—not only used, that is, but also used up.

as ancillary to creation, instrumental to creation, subordinate to and thus other than creation, are in fact forms and modes *of* creation.

The distinction we can retain is a purely quantitative one: the essays show less internal copying that do the journals. This is hardly much of an argument for denying the journal a place in the Emersonian corpus; indeed if we try to understand it in Emerson's terms we find it tends to put the journal at dead center. For though the essays are essentially fluid, and only prudentially and apparently fixed, they tempt the reader to believe otherwise. The journals do not. "In taking up a cotemporary book," writes Emerson, "we forget that we see the house that is building & not the house that is built" (JMN VIII: 132). And still more, it would seem, in taking up a book that has been made by the passage of time to seem not a shanty but a mausoleum.

There remains the distinction between the whole and the part, which has been most vividly formulated by Emerson himself:

> This Book is my Savings Bank. I grow richer because I have somewhere to deposit my earnings; and fractions are worth more to me because corresponding fractions are waiting here that shall be made integers by their addition. (JMN IV: 250–51)

In the model this distinction implies, the journals are a heap of fragments; Emerson the skilled joiner reads through them in search of fragments apt for joining together; once fitted together, and elaborated, the fragments of the journal become the wholes of lectures and essays. Against this model are two arguments, the first intuitive and short, the second speculative and long.

The intuitive argument is that the characteristic utterance in the diary is simply *not* a fragment, not, that is, intrinsically incomplete. James saw this clearly, saying of a journal passage on Webster that it was "not a rough jotting, but, like most of the entries . . . a finished piece of writing."[14] We have only to read a few entries to see it ourselves—starting, perhaps, with the full, rounded, and misleading statement quoted in the previous paragraph. But as this is a sort of epigraph, an undated creed preceding the first of Emerson's mature journals, we might better take some of the briefer paragraphs closely following it:

> The plough displaces the spade, the bridge the watermen, the press the scrivener.

14. James, "Emerson," p. 450.

The moral of your piece should be cuneiform & not polygonal. Judge of the success of the piece by the exclusive prominence it gives to the subject in the minds of all the audience.

To Goethe there was no trifle. Glauber picked up what every body else threw away. Cuvier made much of humblest facts. The lower tone you take the more flexible your voice is. The whole landscape is beautiful though the particulars are not. "You are never are tired whilst you can see far."

Luther & Napoleon are better treatises on the Will than Edwards's. Will does not know if it be cold or hot or dangerous; he only goes on to his mark & leaves to mathematicians to calculate whether a body can come to its place without passing through all the intermediates. "Men have more heart than mind." (JMN IV:253–57)

Should we want other evidence than the immediate judgment of our critical sense, we might note Emerson's rueful account of the obstacles to marshalling these utterances into essays:

Here I sit & read & write with very little system & as far as regards composition with the most fragmentary result: paragraphs incompressible each sentence an infinitely repellent particle.[15]

As indeed is inevitable; created as rounded wholes, such sentences and paragraphs can be fitted together only with difficulty and by main strength. They can be given a place in a larger form and with respect to that larger form are relatively fragments; absolutely fragments, however, intrinsically incomplete, they are not.

The speculative argument against the invidious distinction between whole and part is based on a taxonomy of the Emersonian literary system and, in particular, on a distinction within the corpus of the journals. These are suggestively divided by their most recent, most devoutly erudite, and most astonishingly thorough and rigorous editors into two classes: the regular journals and the miscellaneous notebooks. We can distinguish the classes on two counts: the regular journals are dated and ordered chronologically, the miscellaneous notebooks are not; the miscellaneous notebooks have generally a particular topic or special function, the regular journals do not. The topics and functions vary, of course, hence the legitimate qualification "miscellaneous." Those distinguished by topic include volumes on

15. Joseph Slater, ed., *The Correspondence of Emerson and Carlyle* (New York: Columbia University Press, 1964; henceforth abbreviated CEC), p. 185.

Charles Chauncy Emerson, on Margaret Fuller, on history, on mind; those distinguished by function include lecture notebooks, quotation books, account books. But in all this variety we can hold to the distinction between the topical and the universal; the miscellaneous notebooks are above all *specialized*. They evoke that sad Emersonian example, the farmer who has ceased somehow to be man on the farm, the laborer who has ceased to be a man.

But then comes the refractory fact: at no time does Emerson ever stop using the regular journals for the purposes to which the miscellaneous notebooks are exclusively devoted. When his brother Charles dies, he sets aside a book almost as a memorial to him, transcribing there excerpts from his writings, anecdotes and *mots*, comments and descriptions; but he does not then cease discussing or quoting Charles in the regular journals. He sets aside several books as quotation books, on several plans, but notoriously does not stop recording quotations in the regular journals. He sets aside several books for lecture notes but does not cease to write passages for use in the lectures in the regular journals. At no point, that is, is any function or topic *severed* from the regular journals; these remain a sort of undifferentiated protoplasm, an amoeba occasionally putting out pseudopods. Thus the miscellaneous notebooks are not so much a permanent *redistribution* of the functions of the regular journals as a momentary *crystallization* of them; the topic is identified, the function chosen, but nothing is ever subtracted from the regular journals, which remain, somehow, the whole, undivided and inexhaustible.[16] Again Emerson provides us with a gratifyingly precise image of the journals in this aspect in his portrait of the protean American omni-apprentice:

> A sturdy lad from New Hampshire or Vermont, who in turn tries all the professions, who *teams it, farms it, peddles*, keeps a school, preaches, edits a newspaper, goes to Congress, buys a township, and so forth, in successive years, and always, like a cat, falls on his feet.[17]

16. On the very different relation between sermon and journal in the period of Emerson's ministry, see "Strayings and Temptations," pp. 45–47.

17. "Self-Reliance," W II: 76.

This image is not an Emersonian fantasy but a recognizably American type. William Cobbett writes in 1818 that "besides the great quantity of work performed by the American labourer, his *skill*, the *versatility* of his talent, is a great thing. Every man can use a *axe*, a *saw*, and a *hammer*. Scarcely one who cannot do any job at rough carpentry, and mend a plough or a waggon. Very few indeed, who cannot kill and dress pigs and sheep, and many of them oxen calves. Every farmer is a *neat* butcher; a butcher for *market*; and, of course, 'the boys' must learn. This is a great convenience. It makes you

Now if we keep this taxonomy in mind in thinking not only about the journals but also about the whole Emersonian oeuvre, we will find that the lectures and essays belong in the subordinate category of the topical notebooks. This feels wrong at first, of course; but as we reflect on the irreverent comparison between the secondary journals and the great Emersonian masterpieces, it becomes commandingly plausible. It illuminates, for example, the peculiar nature of Emerson's public titles. Lamb's essays, say, are often ironically titled, the title promising less than the essay gives, the relation between title and topic enigmatic and oblique; Emerson's lectures and essays are titled according to their central topic: not "A Dissertation on Roast Pork" but "Bacon," "History," "Friendship." Montaigne's essay "On Some Verses of Vergil" includes passages on the change from youth to old age, on the remembrance of past pleasures, on virtue and nobility, on the marriage of Socrates and on Montaigne's own; Emerson's essay "Love" gives a series of thoughts on love. Nor is that essay, or any of Emerson's other essays, so shaped by an organizing poetic power as to become essentially forms other than collections. This assertion touches on a vexed question, of course. Much intelligent work has been done to show precisely the contrary. But it has produced no agreement on the nature of Emersonian poetic order and has left intact the powerful statements denying its existence. Of these the most brilliantly sardonic, surprisingly, is Alcott's: "you may begin at the last paragraph and read backwards."[18] The most evocative, however, are Emerson's own:

> In a fortnight or three weeks my little raft [the 1841 *Essays*] will be afloat. Expect nothing more of my powers of construction,—no shipbuilding, no clipper, smack, nor skiff even, only boards and logs tied together. . . . I dot evermore in my endless journal, a line on every knowable in nature; but the arrangement [of the *Essays*] loiters long, and I get a brick-kiln instead of a house.[19]

---

so independent as to a main part of the means of housekeeping. All are *ploughmen*. In short, a good labourer here can do *anything* that is to be done upon a farm" (from Cobbett, *A Year's Residence in The United States of America*, in Allan Nevins, ed., *America Through British Eyes* [New York: Oxford University Press, 1948], p. 66).

18. Alcott, *Concord Days*, cited in Buell, *Literary Transcendentalism*, p. 160.

19. CEC, pp. 291 and 278.

In a November, 1836 letter to Elizabeth Palmer Peabody, Emerson writes, "you express overkind opinions of my little book [*Nature*] but think it wants connexion. I thought it resembled the multiplication table" (L II: 46). See also the letter of March, 1838 to Frederic Henry Hedge (L II: 121) and L II: 463.

Reading the best of the arguments against this assessment, such as Lawrence Buell's, we can say perhaps that boards are put with other boards and logs with logs (or, on occasion, deliberately vice versa); but we cannot by any strategy assimilate the essays to that masterpiece of structural ingenuity, the Yankee clipper, and we will do better thinking of them as the gathering spaces of a brickkiln than as the articulated series of forms-in-functions of a house. If the essays are organized differently from the notebooks, they are still closer in nature to them than they are to the coy, self-reflective associations of a Lamb or the exuberant, relentless argument of a Hazlitt.

Both essay and topical notebook, then, are gatherings of passages extracted from the journal by their common subject matter; and though they can be regarded as wholes with respect to the various journal passages they collect, they can also and no less plausibly be regarded as fragments with respect to the journal as a whole. Now what, in Emerson's scheme of things, is the literary status of a topical collection? The crucial passage occurs in the 1835 lecture on Bacon:

> Bacon's method is not within the work itself, but without. . . . All his work lies along the ground, a vast unfinished city. He did not arrange but unceasingly collect facts . . . his work is therefore somewhat fragmentary. . . . It is a vast collection of proverbs, all wise but the order is much of it quite mechanical, things on one subject being thrown together; the order of a shop and not that of a tree or an animal where perfect assimilation has taken place and all the parts have a perfect unity. . . . Works of this sort . . . are never ended. Each of Shakspear's dramas is perfect, hath an immortal integrity. To make Bacon's works complete, he must live to the end of the world.[20]

The "vast unfinished city" has the charm of all fragments and ruins; the grand conclusion, the vision of the immortal writer laboriously concluding the infinite work, is remarkably attractive. But Emerson's criticism of the principle is no less sharp for his admiration of the project. The order of affinity is simply the order of the shop: "things on one subject . . . thrown together." The "thrown" carries the point of the sentence, the depreciation of this coarse and mechanical classification. And the antithesis, in the sentence around which the para-

---

20. Emerson, "Lord Bacon," EL I: 334–35
Compare with this Emerson's later formulation: "Lord Bacon's Method in his books is of the Understanding, but his sentences are lighted by Ideas" (JMN VIII: 46).

graph turns, is "the order of . . . a tree or an animal where perfect assimilation has taken place and all the parts have a perfect unity."

Emerson cites at this crucial point a work of nature rather than a work of literature not, I think, in a sentimental flight to natural beauty, but in intelligent recourse to a conception of natural order, namely Goethe's, that is happily and almost inevitably translatable from the language of science into the language of art. Let us reconstruct Emerson's sense of that conception so as to apply it to our purposes:

> [Goethe] beholding a plant and seeing . . . a petal in transition from a leaf, exclaimed, And why is not every part of a plant a transformed leaf? a petal is a leaf, a seed is a leaf, metamorphosed, and slow-paced experiment has made good this prophetic vision . . .
>
> The same gifted man walking in the Jews' burying ground in the city of Venice saw a sheep's skull on the ground and was struck with the gradation by which the vertebrae passed into the bones of the head. Instantly he said to himself, the vertebra of the spine is the unit of anatomy; all other parts are merely metamorphoses, degradations, abortions, or enlargements of this. The head was only the uppermost vertebra transformed.[21]

The order of the shop, the order of affinity, is the order of Linnaeus. It is essentially empirical; it looks at the things of the world and divides them by their appearances, but makes no attempt to explain the divisions it passively notes. Hence, for Emerson, the power of the Goethean conceptions. The Goethean system reflects what Emerson explicitly says the Baconian system does not, that is, "a method derived from the mind";[22] having noted the diverse wonders of the world, it finds in them "the order of cause and effect" and so reduces them to unity. Emerson writes in "The Humanity of Science" that the mind desires by "tyrannical instinct" to reduce many ideas to few, and few to one.[23] Not heeding that instinct, the mind ordering by affinity gives us simply *too many* entities and gives them to us as distinct entities rather than as linked facets.

If we then ask what literary form would correspond to the Goethean system, it seems that we would want not a book of essays or a series of lectures on various topics but some form by which the law unifying those topics is articulated and manifested. The various topics

21. Emerson, "The Humanity of Science," EL II: 23–24.
22. EL I: 334.
23. EL II: 23; see on the same subject JMN IV: 289ff and JMN VII: 28.

are so many misleading suggestions, so many strivings "to tear the part from its connexion" (JMN VII: 105) "Love" is identified by its title as *other than* "History," other than "Nature" or "Circles." The journal, the undifferentiated whole, makes no such distinctions. At least negatively, at least potentially, it leaves the reader free of the deception the lectures and essays continually imprint. As contrasted with the order of affinity, the order of occurrence can be described as the juxtaposition of the like and the unlike. The phrase evokes the similes of Donne, though seldom in reading the journal do we experience the quick, intense, cerebral pleasure asociated with the perception of a surprising similarity. Indeed we seldom notice the juxtaposition of any one passage with any other; we notice rather the unity of all with all. We have passages on art, on history, on self-reliance, on the poet, all in immediate succession, and our response is not a perception of how one in particular is related to another in particular but of how all are related to all. We recall at this point Firkins' remark cited earlier:

> The whole fascination of life for Emerson lay in the disclosure of identity in variety, that is, in the concurrence, the *running together*, of several distinct images or ideas.[24]

This disclosure the lectures and essays formally occlude, and the journal formally encourages.[25]

24. Firkins, *Ralph Waldo Emerson* (Boston: Houghton Mifflin, 1915), p. 237.

On this same topic see JMN VII: 102 and Buell's excellent analysis of "The Sphinx" (*Literary Transcendentalism*, p. 182)

25. In this connection Emerson's celebrated account of his 1833 visit to the Jardin des Plantes seems a temporary reconciliation of antitheses. In it Emerson does two things. He celebrates the organization of the museum: "How much finer things are in composition than alone. 'Tis wise in man to make Cabinets. . . . this is philanthropy, wisdom, taste—to form a Cabinet of natural history" (JMN IV: 198–99). He also records a vision of nature: "The Universe is a more amazing puzzle than ever as you glance along this bewildering series of animated forms,—the hazy butterflies, the carved shells, the birds, beasts, fishes, insects, snakes,—& the upheaving principle of life everywhere incipient in the very rock aping organized forms. Not a form so grotesque, so savage, nor so beautiful but is an expression of some property inherent in man the observer,—an occult relation between the very scorpions and man" (199–200).

Now a cabinet is among other things a principle of organization, by which like is put with like. Emerson sees this particular cabinet in 1833, that is, twenty-six years before the publication of Darwin's *Origin of Species*. No grand hypothesis, then, no single idea, is available to make sense of the "amazing puzzle." Like is grouped with like and severed from unlike—that is all, and Emerson's sense of amazement, of bewilderment, is precise and legitimate. But against his bewilderment stands his intuition of continuity, of "the upheaving principle of life everywhere incipient in the very rock," of an "occult relation between the scorpions and man." Nothing in the cabinet itself autho-

The Journals as Artifact

We have, then, two literary *corpora*. We are tempted, perhaps, to compare them with respect to form and theme; but we will do better to describe the journal in these respects by comparing it with works formally more like it. The necessary comparison in this context is rather with respect to audience, that is, the comparison between the journal and the lectures and essays as artifacts and commodities. The goal of the comparison is the statement of certain facts about the journal. But in the course of formulating those statements, certain familiar facts about the lectures and essays will appear in a new light. We are incorporating into a consideration of Emerson the writer certain new data concerning Emerson the diarist, and as Emerson knew, a new fact makes a new system.

Let us begin by contrasting two scenes, two descriptions of diarists in the act of presenting their diaries to readers. The first is Emerson's own, drawn from the cloud-capped towers of the imagination:

> Each young and ardent person writes a diary, in which, when the hours of prayer and penitence arrive, he inscribes his soul. The pages thus written are to him burning and fragrant; he reads them on his knees by midnight and by the morning star; he wets them with his tears; they are sacred. . . . After some time has elapsed, he begins to wish to admit his friend to this hallowed experience, and with hesitation, yet with firmness, exposes the page to his eye. Will they not burn his eyes? (*The Complete Works of Ralph Waldo Emerson* [W] III: 188–89, based on JMN VIII: 123–24)

The second is Bronson Alcott's matter-of-fact account of a talk with Emerson in 1839:

> We [Alcott, Emerson, and John Sullivan Dwight] had some conversation after dinner on high themes: the genesis of Nature, the dependence of the elements of the corporeal and physical world on the Soul, etc. Afterward, a walk to E's favorite haunts.
>
> Dwight left toward evening. After tea we conversed on style, my Conversations, the future. I looked over E's commonplace books.[26]

---

rizes or educates that intuition, which indeed fights against the principle of organization it beholds. It ought to be no surprise then to find Emerson writing soon afterwards that "Linnaeus is already read as the Plato who described Atlantis. A classification is nothing but a Cabinet. The whole remains to be done thereafter" (JMN IV: 282; see further JMN V: 405).

26. Odell Shepard, ed., *The Journals of Bronson Alcott* (Boston: Little, Brown, 1938), p. 126.

There is nothing here of one friend's inviting another to share "a hallowed experience." Indeed Alcott is not at this point Emerson's intimate friend at all; rather he is an acquaintance showing some promise of spiritual kinship. It is at this moment, at the moment of *incipient* friendship, that Emerson often presents his journal. Lidian Emerson was offered the journal when still Lydia Jackson: "will you not honor me, my sibyl, by visiting my lowly study and reading the page."[27] Elizabeth Hoar was still Charles Emerson's fiancée when Emerson offered her a similar invitation, as graceful and distant as a courtier's bow: "My dear Elizabeth: Charles allows me to send you, with the best wishes of the day, my old proverb-book."[28]

We may say, then, that in Transcendentalist Concord showing a journal resembles paying a social call; and, like the call, it is returned. Emerson had read Alcott's 1835 journal in 1836, transcribing passages from it into his own and adding some very judicious comments on Alcott's style; so Emerson's 1839 presentation of his own journal to Alcott was only fair play (JMN V: 167–70). Emerson and Fuller exchange diaries as scholars exchange manuscripts, each drawing from and commenting on the other's.[29] We have even the diary as calling card, as when Charles King Newcomb presents his aloud at a sort of Emersonian soiree:

> just now I have been unusually reminded of your peculiar tastes and vein of thinking [Emerson is writing to his aunt Mary] by the visit here of a youth . . . who read me yesterday largely from his journal, his bold and acute criticism on his readings in literature . . . so naive and colloquial and yet poetic in his expression and illustration that [Elizabeth Hoar] agreed with me in observing the ready resemblance.[30]

On occasion journals are sent through the mail, sometimes to be read not only by the correspondent but also by his or her friends.[31] (Letters

27. L I: 437.
28. L II: 3; Rusk identifies the "proverb-book" as Emerson's journal.
29. For Fuller on Emerson see Joel Myerson, ed., "Margaret Fuller's 1842 Journal," *Harvard Library Bulletin* 21, p. 338 and 340, and L III: 89–90; for Emerson on Fuller, L II: 223. The JMN editors suggest that Caroline Sturgis also took part in this system of exchange (JMN XII: xviii).
30. L III: 64, June 20 and 22, 1842; see also JMN VIII: 178.
31. Alcott writes in May 1836, "On Saturday last, I sent to Mr. Russell, by the Morgan's who now leave me for a month to visit their friends, the preceding sheets of my Journal. I prefer this method of communicating with him, as it acquaints him, from time to time, with my favorite plans, purposes, moods of mind of action; and is a fairer transcript of my life, than any thing else" (Joel Myerson, ed., "Bronson Alcott's 'Journal for 1836,' " *Studies in the American Renaissance* 1978, p. 55).

are treated in much the same way; they arrive in the mail and are passed around like rare and choice magazines.[32]) From here to coterie publication in the *Dial*, with its three hundred subscribers, is a small step, and indeed that step is sometimes taken—"nor Gods nor true persons have secrets," wrote Margaret Fuller while editing the review, and excerpts from Charles Emerson's journal were published there, though posthumously, as were excerpts from Alcott's journal with the author hale and hearty in his forties.[33] Emerson in the journal names four possible audiences: oneself, a friend, a few friends, and God. Clearly the journal is read by the least intimate of these audiences: a comfortable group of friends and colleagues. "I would have my book read," Emerson writes,

> as I have read my favorite books not with explosion & astonishment, a marvel and a rocket, but a friendly & agreeable influence stealing like the scent of a flower or the sight of a new landscape on a traveller. I neither wish to be hated & defied by such as I startle, nor to be kissed and hugged by the young whose thoughts I stimulate. (JMN VIII: 106)

The scene Alcott describes realizes and articulates this desire.

The journal is offered to friends and acquaintances, not to a single friend or lover; but also, obviously, it is offered to friends and not to strangers. Those who read have been invited to read, are known to Emerson and chosen by him. They compose a small and unified world. What they are offered is thus an esoteric text—though not a mystery, no secret scroll guarded by passwords, simply a text for the few, for a band of brothers and sisters. Appropriately, the offering of the journal is a *conversational* gesture. We note in Alcott's account that author and reader inhabit the same room. The moment of reading is typically a tête-à-tête. Emerson offers his journal not so much to a reader as to an interlocutor, at worst to a correspondent, and awaits a response. Nor were responses lacking, such as this of Fuller's: "I have found in his journal two sentences that represent the two sides of his thought. . . . I shall write to him about it."[34]

32. JMN VIII: 180: "When C[hanning] says, 'If I were a Transcendentalist I should not seal my letters,' what does he truly say but that he sees he ought not to seal his letters?"

33. Charles Emerson, "Notes from the Journal of a Scholar," *Dial* 1: 1, July 1840; Alcott, "Days from a Diary," *Dial* 2: 4, April 1842. Fuller's remark is taken from the preface to the Alcott selection.

34. Belle Gale Chevigny, *Margaret Fuller: The Woman and the Myth* (Old Westbury, New York: Feminist Press, 1976), pp. 129–30. On Emerson as a reader of Fuller's journals see L II: 135, 197, 223, and 238–39.

The curious thing is that this audience, and this relation between artist and audience, seem *normative* for Emerson. His neat categorization of possible audiences excludes the indifferent and the hostile; if we read him literally, the real audience of the lectures and essays—the rising middle class of Jacksonian America, the city rather than the neighborhood, the faces the lecturer would see only once, the readers the writer would never see—seems no audience at all. Hence the point of his sharp remark to the Jacksonian enthusiast George Bancroft's boast that an editorial in the *Globe* was read by 300,000 people:

> I only told him then I wished they would write better if they wrote for so many. I ought to have said What utter nonsense to name in *my* ear this *number*, as if that were anything. 3,000 000 [*sic*] such people as can read the Globe with interest are as yet in too crude a state of nonage as to deserve any regard. (JMN V: 462)

Emerson does, to be sure, celebrate oratory and orators, eloquently, repeatedly, and amply; against the text shared between friends might be set the speech or text by which the audience is made the speaker's vessel or organ, to be played on and exalted at will. But the actual relation between the Emerson the lecturer and his audience is in comparison empty, lax, and distant; it is to the ideal relation as Wilhelm Meister's actual effect as an actor is to Goethe's notion, or to Wilhelm's own, of the effects of which an actor was capable. No imperial transaction takes place in the presentation of an Emerson lecture; the predominant emotions of the audience are cerebral interest and amiable respect. The editors of the lectures quote a characteristic remark of Emerson's on ideal oratory: "the end of eloquence is—is it not?—to alter in a pair of hours, perhaps in a half hour's discourse, the convictions and habits of years." But then they go on to note that "the inevitable disappointment of such unworldly hopes hastened [Emerson's] eventual disaffection with the omnibus lecture-series as a form."[35] On occasion, of course, a stronger emotion is evoked; but this is most often an emotion leading the hearer or reader away from the larger and more distant audience into the inner circle. This phenomenon Emerson noted, and indeed celebrated:

35. EL II: xii; the passage of Emerson's quoted is in W VII: 64.
See also the admirable collage of comments on Emerson as lecturer in John McAleer, *Ralph Waldo Emerson: Days of Encounter* (Boston: Little, Brown, 1984), pp. 484–93. See also L II: 460.

I believe I was not wise to volunteer myself to this fever fit of lecturing again. . . . But my joy in friends, those sacred people, is my consolation for the mishaps of the adventure, and they for the most part come to me from this *publication* of myself.[36]

The *telos* of the keenest response of the lecture hearer is precisely the space and role of the journal reader.

A text for friends and not for lovers, in that sense a public text; a text for friends and not for strangers, in that sense an esoteric text; a text offered as and within a speech act, within a human relation, not a text for reception but for reaction; and also, as we see in recalling Alcott's account once again, a text functioning within an outmoded, almost idyllic system of production and exchange. One meaning of "this Book is my Savings Bank" is, "this, and not the Commercial or the Massachusetts, is *my* savings bank"; in fact, the journals resemble not so much a savings bank as the hoarded gold of a thrifty peasant distrustful of the vaults around the corner, available for the use of friends but not for the profiteering of bankers.[37] Emerson's journal is simply shared with Alcott, or exchanged, perhaps, for payment in kind, a journal for a journal. Nor, unlike the book of essays, is the journal part of any of the mechanical, technological, or corporate networks of Emerson's society. Once the book, the pens, and the ink are bought, the production is all Emerson's own.[38] Emerson the diarist requires neither the printing press for production nor the publishing house for distribution; the book he produces is written, not printed; given, not sold; carried, not shipped.

In this respect too the journal seems Emerson's normative text, and the sort of textual performance he does best. As a diarist in Transcendentalist Concord, Emerson is in the thick of things; he reads as many journals as are to be read, and his journal is zestily displayed to as many people as is anyone's else's by all the available media. He is perhaps the most successful of all the Transcendentalist diarists in the Transcendental diaristic economy. He fills the role of

36. CEC, p. 255.

37. Thus Emerson writes to his aunt Mary in August 1827, "all your letters are valuable to me; those most so I think which you esteem the least. I grow more avaricious of this kind of property like other misers with age, and like expecting heirs would be glad to put my fingers into the chest of 'old almanacks' before they are a legacy" (L I: 208).

38. Interestingly in this connection, Emerson gives over the practice of having the volumes of his journal hand-sewn, and begins to buy them ready-made, just at the moment he becomes conscious of them as savings banks, in 1834.

lecturer less fully; he makes, as William Charvat notes, "only the indispensable compromises with his audience."[39] As a lecturer he is the reliable purveyor of a luxury item, never out of fashion but never in it. Similar reservations mark his involvement with his publications. Like the lectures, the books are neither in nor out of fashion, and sell moderately well. But tellingly, Emerson made sure that they would not sell better than moderately by allowing the publishers and distributors he dealt with less than their usual discount on the books' price, and later by "severely [restricting] the advertising of his books—at the very moment when Barnum, Beecher, and Bonner were inventing the modern art of ballyhoo."[40] Emerson was no aesthete denouncing vulgar popularity, indeed he was a lover on principle of great popular success. But in his behavior, he seems far more at home, far more engaged, as the purveyor of a journal than as the seller of a lecture or essay—the *fit* between him and the diarist's role is far closer than that between him and the lecturer's.

Let us return to Alcott's scene one last time to consider the diarist as artisan. Emerson in displaying his journal is not displaying it in its entirety but tailoring a selection from it to the singular sensibility of the particular reader at hand; what one reader gets no other reader will ever get. Similarly, the journal is of course centrally a manuscript, that is, an *unicum*, something resembling a painting rather than the abundantly multiplied artifact of the novel, subject to subtler control and so incapable of wider distribution. Industry can regularize and multiply but not customize. In the journal Emerson retains control of the pagination, and thus of the shape of the page; he can isolate or juxtapose paragraphs at will (and exploits that freedom, emphasizing, say, the brief declaration of his son Waldo's death by leaving it alone on the page, a sentence surrounded by—overwhelmed by—an expanse of white space). He may scribble or write boldly or doodle. He need not observe printers' conventions, which annihilate individual distinctions; he may punctuate and capitalize to shape sentences and to emphasize or to obscure individual words.[41] He can present the journal as the thing that in his belief all texts really are anyway,

39. Charvat, *The Profession of Authorship in America*, Matthew J. Bruccoli, ed. (Columbus: Ohio State University Press, 1968), p. 306.
40. Ibid., p. 293.
41. Thus JMN VII: 150: "With new perception, we shall disburthen our Memory of all its trumpery when we can create." Capitalizing "Memory" gives it a special status interestingly at odds with the proposition in which the word occurs.

the house that is building and not the house that is built, the text as an accretion in time, with its corrections, its deletions, its unresolved alternatives, its first and second thoughts together, its interpolations and erasures: an artisanal text in a premonetary economy, the perfect object of an essentially free and friendly transaction between writer and reader.

Against this we might theoretically set the improvisational freedom of the lecture, or the impeccable beauty of the book; but again, the example of the journal seems normative. The Emersonian lecture, though oral, is *read*. Emerson and Carlyle discuss the point at length in their letters, neither moving an inch from his original disposition, Carlyle steadfastly the improviser and Emerson, knowingly and sometimes sadly, the reader of a text:

> I am always haunted with brave dreams of what might be accomplished in the lecture-room—so free & so unpretending a platform,—a Delos not yet made fast—I imagine an eloquence of infinite variety—rich as conversation can be, with anecdote, joke, tragedy, epics & pindarics, argument & confession. I should love myself wonderfully better if I could arm myself to go, as you go, with the word in the heart & not in a paper.[42]

Hence, presumably, Emerson's vigilant attempts to prohibit reporters from giving full accounts of lectures—he knew that what he said one night he would say the next, and to a hearer who had read the account of the lecture he would have nothing new to say.[43]

Nor does anything in Emerson's work suggest an interest in, a vital, intense response to, the power and beauty of the book—nothing, say, to match the spiritualized classification of book sizes Melville used to create a taxonomy of whales. Emerson was not indifferent to the look of a book, and attended with surprising care to the layout of the *Dial;* but when *Nature* came out in 1836 with the first sentences of the essays printed as mottoes, Emerson was only mildly annoyed, and comforted himself easily enough with the remark that "a good sentence can never be put out of countenance by any blunder of compositors."[44]

A text for acquaintances and not for lovers; a text for friends and not

---

42. CEC 308; see also Oliver Wendell Holmes's remarks on Emerson's difficulties with impromptu oratory in Cabot, *Memoir* 2: 621–22.

43. Cabot writes that Emerson objected even "to the taking of private notes" (*Memoir* II: 669).

44. JMN V: 190; see also Emerson's occasional disparaging comments on book composition, e.g., JMN VII: 358 and 404–405, and L II: 381.

for strangers; an esoteric text, conversational rather than intimate, social rather than solitary, domestic rather than oratorical; a text for sharing, and not for selling; a craftsman's text in the midst of the nineteenth century's astounding mechanical reproduction of works of art: these are the principal traits of the journal *qua* commodity and artifact.

Emerson and his Diaristic Circle

Two of his Emerson's diaristic traditions, the Lockean commonplace book and its diametric opposite the Moodyan diary, we have already considered in describing the process by which Emerson found his form; and in that description, as in most descriptions of the relation between an innovative artist and his or her tradition, we proceeded as if the traditions were originals and Emerson's response to them a creative translation. We posited, that is, the traditions as things given, and Emerson's development of them as something free, something by which the things given were enhanced and augmented. But there is of course another pertinent tradition also, the tradition of the Transcendentalist journal, and another way of thinking about Emerson's relation with it. Here we should rather conceive of Emerson as the original, and the tradition as a collective translation of him; for Emerson is after all the central Transcendentalist, and in speaking of the Transcendentalist journal we are speaking of a collection of journals by people very much subject to his influence, though in varying degrees and manners.

The results of this second investigation are strikingly regular. All the Transcendentalist journals share with Emerson's the central innovation we discussed earlier, the combination of Moodyan diary and Lockean commonplace book; but all of them—with the exception of Thoreau's, which early in its development takes to itself the single and exhaustive function of recording nature[45]—*conventionalize* the formal invention Emerson devised. It is true, of course, that the principal Transcendentalist journals are, like their authors, stubborn individualists: Fuller's is the diametric opposite of Thoreau's, a brilliant account of social interactions; Hawthorne's is an exercise book in scene painting; Alcott's is in diligence if not in gusto almost Pepysian,

45. This is the convincing argument of Cameron, *Writing Nature*.

faithfully recording the events of the day, reflections upon them, and so to bed.[46] But as we compare Emerson's journal with these journals of his colleagues, his neighbors, his friends, we find that these latter are associated with one another, and differentiated from Emerson's, by certain large formal traits: their strict adherence to the rhythm of the calendar; the prevalence in them of a form of entry in which narration precedes reflection; and the prevalence in them of the first and third grammatical persons, and the relative scarcity of the second. Or, more loftily: the telling points of comparison between Emerson and the Transcendentalist journal bear on the diarist's relation to time, the relation between thought and its occasion, and the relation between speaker and audience. In each of these aspects the diaries of Emerson's Transcendentalist colleagues resemble more closely than does Emerson's the general Western diaristic pattern, if we can indeed speak of such a pattern. But more important for our present purpose is that it is Emerson's formal innovations, and not the flattening out of them performed by his colleagues, that we can make sense of as intelligent responses to the America with which the Transcendentalists had so equivocal a relation. John Jay Chapman wrote that

46. For Thoreau see Bradford Torrey and Francis H. Allen, eds., *The Journal of Henry D. Thoreau* (Boston: Houghton Mifflin, 1906); this is gradually being superseded by the edition of the journal being made as part of the Santa Barbara edition of the complete works. For Fuller see Joel Myerson, ed., "Margaret Fuller's 1842 Journal"; the edited selections from Fuller's journal in the *Memoirs of Margaret Fuller Ossoli* are to be presumed untrustworthy. For Alcott see Myerson, ed., "Bronson Alcott's 'Journal for 1836,'" and also Larry Carlson, ed., "Bronson Alcott's 'Journal for 1837,'" *Studies in the American Renaissance* 1981: 27–132 and 1982: 53–117; also Shepard's selection from the journal for periods not covered by these editions. For Hawthorne see Randall Stewart, ed., *The American Notebooks* (New Haven; Yale University Press, 1932).

Other, wildly diverse journals of approximately the same circle: Robert F. Lucid, ed., *The Journal of Richard Henry Dana, Jr.* (Cambridge: Harvard University Press, 1968); Donald Yannella and Kathleen Malone Yannella, eds., "Evert A. Duyckinck's 'Diary: May 29–November 8, 1847,'" in *Studies in the American Renaissance* 1978, pp. 207–58; Guy R. Woodall, "The Journals of Convers Francis," ibid 1981, pp. 265–343, and 1982, pp. 227–84; Francis B. Dedmond, ed., "Christopher Pearse Cranch's 'Journal. 1938,'" ibid. 1983, pp. 129–49; Frank Shuffelton, ed., "The Journal of Evelina Metcalf," ibid. 1984, pp. 29–46; Judith Kennedy Johnson, ed., *The Journals of Charles King Newcomb* (Providence: Brown University Press, 1946); and Kenneth Walter Cameron's edition of Franklin Benjamin Sanborn's journal in *The Transcendental Climate*.

Obviously, the history of the Transcendentalist journal has not yet been written, and the present account offers a description only of such traits of that journal as help to make sense of Emerson's.

"if a soul be taken and crushed by democracy till it utter a cry, that cry will be Emerson."[47] The comparison between Emerson and his diaristic colleagues reveals the care Emerson took to give that cry a fitting form.

Most of the Transcendentalists, idlers and Bohemians as they may have seemed, kept remarkably regular diaries: day follows day with few gaps and hardly any anomalies, and Alcott, the chief eccentric of the lot, is as punctual a diarist as John Quincy Adams. Emerson by contrast seems an idler. His journal G, for examples, is marked "1841" on its cover. The next date, July 6, 1841, occurs on page ten, after nine pages of parables and *aperçus*. On page thirteen we get the notation "Sunday"; on page eighteen, "Nantasket Beach: 10 July." Then nothing till "27 Aug." on page sixty-two; then, on page eighty, "Aug. 31." Perhaps, of course, Emerson wrote more often than he dated; forty-four typescript pages between one date and the next seem too great a work for a single day, and for all we know he made an entry a day throughout his life. But he did not *date* regularly, and the formal consequences are considerable. He was also given to keeping multiple volumes of his regular journal at a time— that is, not differentiating them by function, as he differentiates the regular journals from the topical notebooks or as Hawthorne differentiates his chronicles from his waste book, but simply going between one volume of the regular journal and another, sometimes between one volume and several others, all devoted to the same purpose.[48] Sometimes he makes "double-enders," that is, abandons a journal for a while and then returns to it, creating a book of two opposed irregular sequences, one from the front and the other from the back.[49] Once he keeps a volume exclusively from back to front; infrequently, but often enough for the practice to seem symptomatic

47. Chapman, "Emerson," in Edmund Wilson, ed., *The Shock of Recognition* (New York: Grosset & Dunlap, 1955), 1: 657.
48. See "Strayings and Temptations," pp. 51–53 on the multiplicity of the 1833–1834 travel notebooks.
These anomalies vary in frequency of occurrence over time, and as we have seen, on at least one occasion of their more frequent occurrence they express and resolve some particular difficulty. In this context, however, the point is that the practice is in general *acceptable* to Emerson, is consistent with his sense of what it was to keep a journal as it was not for his diaristic colleagues.
49. On double-enders see also "The Loss of Form," n. 6, p. 142.

rather than accidental, he places dated entries out of chronological sequence.[50]

We can read these practices both philosophically and politically. On the one hand, the irregular sequence of dates creates a book not so much of days as of events.[51] "Beware the sounds of singlehearted Time/ For they will chill thee like the hoarfrost's rime," writes William Ellery Channing (JMN VIII: 352); in Emerson's journal, time is not *chronos* but *kairos*. The dated entries recording Ellen's and Waldo's deaths bring the journal into charged time; the undifferentiated flow of duration has been punctuated by a date that is also a *fact*. In this context it is Alcott and Adams who seem idlers, passively submitting to the empty order of the calendar; and Emerson by contrast seems for a moment to resemble Coleridge's man of methodical industry, who "realizes [time's] ideal divisions, and gives a character and individuality to its moments."[52]

But the universal pressure of time is in every individual case felt as the pressure of a particular civilization; and we may do better here to think not of a philosophical rebellion against Wordsworth's "melancholy space and doleful time," against the human condition, but of a principled, local rebellion against the pressure of what Emerson calls "our national hurry."[53] We may give this argument some weight by envisioning the national scene in which the diary functions and against which it rebels, trying to catch in pointillistic images something as insubstantial as the tempo of a nation: Dickens's first conversation in America, begun with stunning appropriateness by his learning the unfamiliar American idiom "right away," Mrs. Trollope's warning that the boarder who does not "rise exactly in time to reach the boarding table at the hour appointed for breakfast . . . will get a stiff bow from the lady president, cold coffee, and no egg." Basil Hall brilliantly describes an early example of that work of American genius, the fast-food restaurant:

50. A good example is the swatch of poems in JMN III: 289–95, the first dated July 6, 1831, amidst October entries of the same year, the remainder undated, including *gnothi seauton*.

51. Compare Boerner, *Tagebuch*, p. 12: "the curve of the diary leads from day to day, the curve of the chronicle from event to event."

52. "On Method," from *The Friend*, in I. A. Richards, ed., *The Portable Coleridge* (New York: Penguin, 1977), p. 341. The whole section is in one of its aspects a warning against the dangers of the calendrical diary.

53. L II: 398.

We entered a long, narrow, and rather dark room, or gallery, fitted up like a coffee-house, with a row of boxes on each side made just large enough to hold four persons, and divided into that number by fixed arms limiting the seats. Along the passage, or avenue, between the rows of boxes, which was not above four feet wide, were stationed sundry little boys, and two waiters, with their jackets off—and a good need, too, as will be seen. At the time we entered, all the compartments were filled except one, of which we took possession. There was an amazing clatter of knives and forks; but not a word audible to us was spoken by any of the guests. This silence, however, on the part of the company, was amply made up for by the rapid vociferations of the attendants, especially of the boys, who were gliding up and down, and across the passage, inclining their heads first to one box, then to another, and receiving the whispered wishes of the company, which they straightway bawled out in a loud voice, to give notice of what fare was wanted. It quite boggled my comprehension to imagine how the people at the upper end of the room, by whom a communication was kept up in some magical way with the kitchen, could contrive to distinguish between one order and another. It was still more marvellous that within a few seconds after our wishes had been communicated to one of the aforesaid urchins, imps, gnomes, or whatever name they deserve, the things we asked for were placed piping hot before us. It was really quite an Arabian Nights' Entertainment, not a sober dinner at a chop-house. . . .

There could not be, I should think, fewer than a dozen boxes, with four people in each; and as everyone seemed to be eating as fast as he could, the extraordinary bustle may be conceived. We were not in the house above twenty minutes, but we sat out two sets of company at each.[54]

But the best example of American hurry is perhaps the American newspaper—that shockingly concrete and lengthy chronicle of the time, that public "journal" of exemplary regularity, regulated by, indeed almost a manifestation of, the mechanical succession of days. This image of calendrical time was among the commonest American possessions, and surely the most intently scrutinized American text. Tocqueville notes "the astonishing circulation of letters and newspapers in the midst of these wild forests"; Anthony Trollope, though a

54. Dickens, *American Notes*, in Andrew Lang, ed., *The Works of Charles Dickens* (New York: Scribner, 1900) 28: 27; Frances Trollope, *Notes on the Domestic Manners of the Americans*, ed. Donald Smalley (New York: Vintage, 1949), p. 283; Hall, *Travels in North America in the Years 1827 and 1828*, in Nevins, *America Through British Eyes*, pp. 111–12.

more judicious writer than his flamboyant and brilliant mother, declares that "to men, and to women also, in the United States [newspapers] may be said to be the one chief necessary of life." When Martin Chuzzlewit arrives in New York, the newsboys are crying their wares before his whip touches the shore:

> "Here's this morning's New York Sewer!" cried one. "Here's this morning's New York Stabber! Here's the New York Family Spy! Here's the New York Private Listener! Here's the New York Peeper! Here's the New York Plunderer! Here's the New York Keyhole Reporter! Here's the New York Rowdy Journal! Here's all the New York Papers!"[55]

Dickens the satirist heightens the *character* of the press; Dickens the realist notes the sheer volume and diversity of its productions, and its universal intrusiveness.

Against such compulsive regularity, against the pressure of the day so sharply imprinted by the daily newspaper, Emerson's irregularities seem a sort of principled idleness: a quiet attempt to realize the American *flâneur*. This was, as Walter Benjamin noted in commenting on Poe's "The Man of the Crowd," an almost impossible task:

> The pressure [of the crowd] has a still more dehumanizing effect in that in Poe only human beings are referred to in discussing it. When the movement of the crowd is slowed, the cause is not that vehicular traffic interrupts it; vehicular traffic is never mentioned. The cause is rather that one crowd blocks another. In a mass of such a nature, Bohemian idleness [die Flanerie] was unlikely to yield much fruit.[56]

55. Tocqueville in George Wilson Pierson, *Tocqueville and Beaumont in America* (New York: Oxford University Press, 1938), p. 588; Anthony Trollope, *North America* (New York: Knopf, 1951), ed. Donald Smalley and Bradford Allen Booth, p. 501; Dickens, *Martin Chuzzlewit*, in Lang, ed., *The Works of Dickens*, 10: 271.
One more passage for good measure, from Mrs. Trollope: "every *American newspaper* is more or less a magazine, wherein the merchant may scan while he holds out his hand for an invoice, 'Stanzas by Mrs. Hemans,' or a garbled extract from Moore's Life of Byron; the lawyer may study his brief faithfully, and yet contrive to pick up the valuable dictum of some American critic, that 'Bulwer's novels are decidedly superior to Sir Walter Scott's;' nay, even the auctioneer may find time, as he bustles to his tub, or his tribune, to support his pretensions to polite learning, by glancing his quick eye over the columns, and reading that 'Miss Mitford's descriptions are indescribable.' If you buy a yard of ribbon, the shop-keeper lays down his newspaper, perhaps two or three, to measure. I have seen a brewer's dray-man perched on the shaft of his dray and reading one newspaper, while another was tucked under his arm" (Trollope, *Domestic Manners*, p. 93).
56. Benjamin, *Charles Baudelaire: ein Lyriker im Zeitalter des Hochkapitalismus*, in Rolf Tiedemann and Hermann Schweppenhaeuser, eds., *Walter Benjamin: Gesammelte Schriften* (Frankfurt: Suhrkamp, 1980), I:2: 556.

Perhaps Emerson found in the journal the only refuge in America from what Marx called America's "Feverishly adolescent movement of material production."[57] Participation in the Concord cottage industry of journal keeping may be construed as a partial rejection of American mechanical and mercantile capitalism; this diaristic suggestion of a deliberately unsystematic, irregular, almost dilatory relation to calendrical time seems a partial rejection of American tempo, of its *conception* of time, its adaptation of human rhythms to the rhythms of clock and calendar and bell.

"A creation is a production from nothing," wrote Kierkegaard; "the occasion is, however, the nothing from which everything comes."[58] This of course leaves to the taste and strategy of the individual writer the choice of how to *present* the relation between occasion and creation. In most of the Transcendentalist diaries, the individual entries are ordered from dross to gold—from, that is, the bare facts of a lived day to the truths rooted in it and flowering from it. Not in Emerson's, however; his utterances seem to arise *ex nihilo*, altogether severed, to use another phrase of Kierkegaard's, from the umbilical cord of their original mood.[59]

> I have read little this week. Indeed, my practice in this respect is faulty. I should read more than I have done during the past year. The thoughts of the mighty are not familiar as I would have them. Little, and little drippings from petty intellects, surely I do not court, nor catch; yet I am, by far, too much alone for hardy growth, or graceful ease. Books are always at one's elbow, and, well selected, ever give counsel and encouragement. . . .[60]

> Everything good, we say, is on the highway. A virtuoso hunts up with great pains a landscape of Guercino, a crayon sketch of Salvator, but the Transfiguration, The Last Judgment, the Communion, are on the walls of the Vatican where every footman may see them without price. You have got for 500 pounds an autograph receipt of Shakspeare; but for nothing a schoolboy can read Hamlet . . . I think I will never read any but the commonest of all books. (Emerson JMN VIII: 284–85)

57. As cited ibid., p. 555.
58. As quoted in J. P. Stern, *Lichtenberg: A Doctrine of Scattered Occasions* (Bloomington: Indiana University Press, 1959), p. 53.
59. As quoted in Boerner, *Tagebuch*, p. 24.
60. Alcott, "Diary for 1836," p. 40.

Cut an entry of Alcott's in two, and the second half will be much like Emerson's; add to Emerson's the occasion that prompted it, and it will seem much like Alcott's; but Alcott always joins, and Emerson always severs.[61]

The immediate temptation is to say that Emerson's journal is a deliberately *purer* book, more ethereal, more inaccessibly shielded in the ivory tower: thoughts stripped of facts. Much in our traditional sense of Emerson strengthens that temptation. Margaret Fuller's forthright declaration may stand for the judgments of his contemporaries:

> [Emerson] does not care for facts, except so far as the immortal essence can be distilled from them. He has little sympathy with mere life: does not seem to see the plants grow, merely that he may rejoice in their energy.[62]

The JMN editors are more circumspect; but are they not possessed by the same idea?

> On the theory that some factual details, though tedious in quantity and isolation, have a certain contrasting interest or usefulness when scattered about among the real products of Emerson's mind, [we] have included many of them. (JMN I: 37)

"If a man will kick a fact out of the window," Emerson writes, "when he comes back he finds it again in the chimney corner" (JMN VIII: 306). Obviously the real production of Emerson's mind is the *whole:* is what it produced, and in fact Emerson's journals actually contain much more in the way of unimproved fact than do those of his colleagues: expenditures, lists of books, quotations recorded without comment, bare names, names with the corresponding dates of birth and death, *memoranda.* "The unconquered facts, they draw me" he wrote (JMN VIII: 341); and they did. He felt no obligation, to be sure, to root his truths in facts; but equally little to make his facts flower into truths. The thoughts are there; the facts are there also. But their relations are not determined, not specified; they are not made components of a small intelligible form linking them, but left independent and suspended.

Thus he writes one day, "G. Minot told me he gave 310 dollars for

61. Stern, *Lichtenberg*, p. 53, distinguishes between aphorisms and reflections on the ground that reflections characteristically recount their occasions while aphorisms characteristically suppress it. On Emerson as aphorist, see "The Journal and the Aphorism Book," pp. 113–17.

62. Fuller, "1842 Journal," p. 330.

his field and Peter How gave 140 dollars for his triangle" (JMN VII: 28–29). Then follows a rhapsody on fact:

> Day creeps after day each full of facts—dull, strange, despised things that we cannot enough despise,—call heavy, prosaic, & desart. And presently the aroused intellect finds gold & gems in one of these scorned facts, then finds that the day of facts is a rock of diamonds, that a fact is an Epiphany of God, that on every fact of his life he should rear a temple of wonder, joy, & praise, that in going to eat meat; to buy, or sell; to meet a friend; or thwart an adversary; to communicate a piece of news or buy a book; he celebrates the arrival of an inconceivably remote purpose & law at last on the shores of Being, & into the ripeness & term of Nature. And because nothing chances, but all is locked & wheeled & chained in Law, in these motes & dust he can read the writing of the True Life & of a startling sublimity.

Alcott would have chosen a fact more amenable to spiritualization; Emerson's is stubbornly recalcitrant to it. Alcott would have gone directly from the amenable fact to its *particular* spiritualization. Emerson proceeds from the recalcitrant fact to a celebration of spiritualization in general; the unconquered fact is not spiritualized but set within the field of spirit. Alcott offers a quick and precise but perhaps narrow interpretation, Emerson a slow but insistent exhortation to interpretation at leisure. Alcott practices a small intelligible form, the bipartite entry complete within itself. Emerson draws the reader to a consideration of the journal as a whole, in which these small transactions among neighbors become exemplary not of particular spiritual propositions but of the great facts of Number, Neighborhood, and Commerce.

We can get a different view of this distinction by considering an analogue to it, in the practice of the Puritan diarists of spiritual experiences.[63] These were remarkable precisely by their affinity with Emerson's colleagues and present antagonists; their diaries, like Alcott's, are distinguished by their disposition to record process rather than result. That is: say that one afternoon a Puritan diarist is consumed with envy at his neighbor's good fortune and becomes conscious of that passion. Sitting down that evening to his diary, he may record either the passion or the act of consciousness. The Puritan diarists of spiritual experiences chose with remarkable regularity to record, not

63. For a fuller account of this practice see my "Cotton Mather as Diarist," *Prospects* 8 (1983), pp. 131–33.